# REALITY Vs EXPECTATION

## THE HOME ED GUIDE YOU DIDN'T KNOW YOU NEEDED

Reality Vs. Expectation

Published by Elen Morrigan

Layout and cover design: Elen Morrigan

Printed by Kindle Direct Publishing

ISBN 979-8-857-77120-4

# Contents

**To my children:**

**For always being compassionate, kind teachers despite the ineptitude of their student.**

# Introduction

One day you are doom scrolling the interweb looking at home education curricula that promise they aren't a workbook (they are) and are guides for an interest led autonomous approach (they're not. Seriously, why do we do this to ourselves?) The next you are writing that book you've been meaning to write for several years. In fairness to past me, present me is glad it's taken me several years, because now I have so much more to talk to you about!

In this book we are going to go on a journey together exploring the expectations vs reality of home education. Spoiler - I'm a neurodivergent woman, with an alphabet soup of neurodivergence in my family so this won't be your bog standard 'How to Home Ed book'. There will be pit stops to catch your breath, snack stops and most importantly, opportunities to reflect and soak it all in. This journey will sometimes be like a gentle rolling summer hill, with meadow flowers and sunshine and like an unforgiving snowy ice shelf, threatening to drop you into the abyss, in others and I'm not going to apologise, as that's just how it is with unlearning and relearning as an adult, stick with it. You've got this!

You see, this book is an educational journey, only it's not for your children, it's for you. I'm pretty sure I can already hear you groaning from here! After all, you already went to school for 12+ years. Why on earth do you need to do more learning now? Well, it's exactly because you went to school that we need to traverse the pages of this book together! Ultimately, this is the book I wish I had when I started home education. It's not a ready-made curriculum for children, but a ready-made guide to everything I feel you need to know or explore, from what I've learnt and explored, so far. You'll notice that I said, so far. That's because nearly 10 years into our home education journey, I still have so much to learn. You'll also notice I said, 'ready-made guide' instead of 'ready-made how to'. That's because there is not one specific way to do home education. The laws are blurry, the guidelines that are supposed to interpret those blurry laws are contradictory and the approaches to home education are wide and far reaching. Because of these points, this is a guide on what I wish I had known, from the perspective of this one individual home educator, doing their own thing in England (Aka me!).

Ah yes, who actually am I? I am first and foremost a fellow human being who loves food, dancing and singing badly in the shower. I have a passion for learning, development, and psychology. In a previous life I ran a business, focused on supporting fellow mothers to find balance in their challenging lives. I closed my business to focus more deeply on my children's needs and my own, after a late but timely diagnosis of autism. I have home educated all 4 of my children at various points and currently home educate the youngest 2. The youngest has never been to school, the second youngest left school at 6, their older sibling left at 7 and then returned to school at 11 until the end of compulsory school age and the eldest left school at 11 and was home educated until the end of compulsory school age. Quite the mixed bag as you can imagine! I host a home education podcast called HEFA - The heart of home education and have volunteered my time on forums worldwide as both a home educator and mental health mentor for around 9 years, most recently as an admin on the largest home ed Facebook support group: H.E.F.A Home Education For All. I have been writing about parenting, women's mental health and spirituality for around 15 years and specifically about home education for the past 8 years. This book is a culmination of so many of those things; home education, parental needs, balance but most of all, humanness.

So, without further ado, let's get into it. I've laid the book out in a specific way. Within many of the chapters there is a concept or subject being discussed, the expectation vs reality, my thoughts on it, pit stops for taking a breather and reflecting and then suggestions and activities to support you. This means that you can jump around the chapters of the book however you need to, referencing back to various concepts or reading it through as a whole. Just as there is not one specific way to do home education, there is also not one specific way to work with this book, which starts as we mean to go on. Clever right?

It's probably worth mentioning that I cannot possibly cover everything about home ed in this book and I don't intend to. This is about my experiences and what I've learnt, so I will show bias towards home education, I will probably whine a few million times about the school system, and I will most certainly wax lyrical about unschooling and deschooling and self-directed learning. I can guarantee that some of you will read this and feel affronted or even outraged that something you were expecting isn't included. I definitely won't have included enough about structured home education or given a positive enough spin on highly gifted academic-based home education. I get it. I really do. But the title of the book gives you a clue. Those grumbles are your expectations showing, not mine. The reality is that while I'm happy to point you in a vague general direction relating to structured home ed, this book is about what I, a neurodivergent home ed mum of neurodivergent children, felt I needed to know, rather than what 100,000 other people might want me to include.

But I really do hope you'll read it anyway, as you never know what you might take away from it!

Enjoy!

### *Elen Morrigan*

# Choosing home education

Before we start, I want to kick off this chapter with a note on the terminology of home education. I know, know something to learn straight out of the gate! But it's important to me and something I wish someone had taken the time to explain to me when I first became home ed. Elective Home Education is the correct and accurate term for home education in the UK and is a term that veteran home educators fought the government to be used as the preferred term by the DfE. Elective Home Education is often referred to as home education, home ed, home edders and EHE. These all represent Elective Home Education.

Home Schooling is a different term and has a much longer history with origins in America, before becoming a popular term in the UK to describe children being taught at home many years ago. This was then changed to better reflect the educational journey that children who do not use the school system go on. There are specific issues with the use of the term homeschooling that I've come to understand over the years and I'm going to lay them out here in the hopes that you might gain some insight into why me and other home educators are protective of the term 'Elective Home Education or Home Ed'. Let's explore them now.

**1. Evolving language matters**.

Since the Covid Pandemic, Homeschooling has taken on a separate meaning in England, to mean education provided by a school to a pupil still enrolled in a school, but who is currently at home.

## 2. Words in general matter.

Education is a human right for every child and part of a parent's legal responsibility in the UK. Schooling is not the same thing. Schooling is an optional way in which you can become educated.

## 3. Definitions matter.

Schooling is a method of instruction and training; the act of being taught in a school. The definition of a school is a place where children go to be educated. Education is a body of knowledge acquired by a person. (In a range of ways of which schooling can be one)

## 4. Perception matters

Because of words and definitions homeschooling can imply to others that you are providing 'school at home'. It leads to a perception of a school room set up at home, with desks and a teacher and a school curriculum and timetables.

## 5. Representation matters

When we represent home education as homeschooling, we tell stakeholders such as the local authority to expect school-at-home practices. By the very use of 'school' being used to represent home education, we erode other valid and respected approaches to education that exist and ask the local authority to judge us by a school-based education.

## 6. Education matters

The word education has become synonymous with the word school and with it a push to see anything outside of school-based practice as 'wrong'. The words home education challenge this and remind us that education happens in many forms, only one of which is 'school'.

## 7. Mindset matters

When you look at how ingrained the word school has become in relation to education, using 'school' to describe your own home education can block your mindset and prevent you from seeing all of the ways that learning can happen. Education provides us with an expanding perspective. Schooling provides us with a restricted perspective.

## 8. Media matters

The media use the term homeschooling on purpose to compare the education of home educators, to that of schooled children. They also use it to compare home education to that of 'education other than at school' (EOTAS) where a child is provided education by the local authority - this conflates the two and lumps very different education as one. These styles and approaches to education are not comparable but by using the word 'school' it implies they are all the same things.

## 9. Expert judgement matters

Experts such as doctors, education psychologists, social workers and local authorities are often called to give evidence in areas relating to children and education. Many do not know and have not been trained to know the laws, the difference between home education and homeschooling and the varying valid approaches to education. So will give evidence based on their own unconscious bias towards a school-at-home approach. Their ignorance of the differences, the laws and the words that protect our community can be devastating for families.

The word education rather than schooling, can and does change lives and home-educated children deserve protection against school-based standards.

Okay now that's out of the way, having supported home educators and been friends with many for nearly 10 years, I can confidently advise that nothing terrifies me more than asking the words *"What made you choose home education?"*. This question elicits a wide range of emotive responses ranging from excitedly proclaiming the wonderful benefits of a certain learning approach, through to snorts of anger and frustration while clarifying it wasn't a choice and everything in between, so wherever you are on that particular journey, I promise it's okay.

Given the state of the education system in 2023, I genuinely found the title of this chapter a little too close to the bone but here we are. It's called Elective Home Education and unless you've been illegally off rolled, you will have elected to home educate to whatever extent you are currently exploring the truth of. While there are of course families who choose home education from the outset, (one of my children is home educated as a first choice) for many, home education is becoming less about choice and more about necessity. A significant number of parents are choosing to home ed for reasons they would consider negative, rather than due to the positive benefits of home education. Sadly, this growing number of families end up in home education because they feel they have no other option. Their child is struggling with several elements of the school system, be those specific needs not being met, medical needs, mental health issues, bullying or issues accessing the curriculum, and that leads to home ed feeling less of a choice and more of an 'out of viable options' situation. With that said, this doesn't mean that those families fail to develop a wonderful provision. It might surprise you to know that regardless of the reason families come to home education, an overwhelming majority end up staying in home education because they actually find it provides a better education, connection and autonomy for their child and family, compared to the alternatives.

*Why are people choosing home education?*

A good percentage of families choose home education because they feel it's the best educational opportunity for their child and despite us coming to home ed for negative reasons initially, it being best, was the exact reason we chose home ed as a first choice for our subsequent youngest child. For many families home ed is a natural extension of parenting. It's a parent's duty to ensure their child receives an education and so they want to provide a bespoke, individualised, and connective education as a part of that parenting and without the interruptions that school education creates simply by design. As I noted previously, home education is also chosen for reasons more connected to negative reasons associated with schooling. Recent results of a survey I provided for a general home educating support community (May 2023, The Home Education For All Facebook group) came back with a whopping 68% citing their reasons as SEN / mental health / medical needs or schools failing the child and leaving the parent with no other options. Home education as a positive 1st choice came in at 12%. Research compiled by the home education charity, Education Otherwise most recently found that -

*45.63% of parents referred to negative reasons relating to schools as their initial primary reason for home-educating their children. This included General dissatisfaction with the school system (21.21%), the school curriculum not being relevant or suitable (9.25%), the school being unable to meet the child's special needs (10.79%) and bullying at school (4.38%) Positive reasons for initially choosing to EHE a child were cited by 30.87% of respondents*[1]

I could write a whole other book on the injustices and shocking state of accessible and inclusive education but for now, let's touch on health via some data from the Good Childhood Report and the NHS mental health of children and young people survey. These are both surveys focusing on

---

[1]England: why parents choose home education." Education Otherwise, 17 August 2020
https://www.educationotherwise.org/england-why-parents-choose-home-education

the mental health and happiness of our young people in the UK.

First up, The Good Childhood Report 2022

*'In 2019-20 (the most recent wave of Understanding Society), happiness with school and schoolwork declined significantly with age and was significantly lower among children in lower income households. Children with a long-term health problem or disability were also significantly less happy with school...'*

*'...In 2022, a larger proportion of children (aged 10 to 17 in the UK) completing The Children's Society's annual household survey were unhappy with school than with the nine other well-being domains they were asked about...'*

*'...Children with a long-term illness or a disability were more likely than other children to be bullied physically (25% compared to 14%) and in other ways (44% compared to 30%).'*

*'Of the seven items asking children about their happiness with specific aspects of school, happiness with how much they were listened to at school was most strongly related to their happiness with school in general. Almost 1 in 5 did not think they had a say in decisions that were important to them in school and more girls and children in key stages 3 and 4 (i.e., in secondary school) reported feeling this way.* [2]

---

[2] The Good Childhood Report 2022." The Children's Society, 22 September 2022

The good childhood report found that school was such a high factor in children's unhappiness that they dedicated an entire chapter to it in their 2022 report compared to other factors.

On to the NHS. In 2017 the NHS ran a survey on the mental health of children and young people. They repeated this survey in 2020, 2021 and 2022. The survey snapshots have not been great. *In 2017 1 in 9 children between the ages of 7 and 16 experienced symptoms that would probably meet the criteria for a mental health disorder. This figure became 1 in 6 by 2022.*

*For young people between 17 and 19 years old this was 1 in 10 at the 2017 survey, with the 2022 survey finding rates as high as 1 in 4.* [3]

For me, these two reports, coupled with home education data, casts a worrying shadow on the current state of the school system and goes some way towards better understanding the motivations of parents deregistering and parents simply choosing to stay opted out in the first place. Parents are experiencing the standard challenges with parenting, but it is now coupled with the most unhappy and mentally unwell generation of children and young people in

https://www.childrenssociety.org.uk/information/professionals/resources/good-childhood-report-2022.

[3] NHS mental health of children and young people survey https://digital.nhs.uk/data-and-information/publications/statistical/mental-health-of-children-and-young-people-in-england

a long time and for many of those children, school is the biggest factor creating those issues.

*The freedom of information*

In an idealistic world that lives inside my head, my expectation is that all parents are made aware of the educational choices available to them. This freedom of information empowers parents to consider the real-world possibilities for their child's educational journeys, with information provided on state schools, academies, independent and private schools, and home education, so that parents can consider all options and make an informed choice. Contrary to what many would have you think, it is parents who best know their children and being aware of the available options and choosing that which most closely suits your child's needs could reduce so much trauma and disengagement from learning in the next generation but instead, the reality is very different.

Currently the status quo is that when a child reaches around three, most parents receive an application pack advising them that it's now time to apply for school. Many children who have not attended nursery or preschool still manage to get this ominous application pack dropped through the door too, thanks to linked up services such as health services. The wording on this paperwork is authoritative and formal and for those not in the know, you really do get the impression that it's something you must do, with an air of unspoken consequences if you fail to do so. In truth it's just an invitation to opt into a service but do they tell you that? Of course not! If you are anything like me, you remember filling these forms out and then sitting while you eagerly await school space allocation day months later, hoping for your first choice. I personally have filled these forms in three times. 2006, 2010 and 2011. What I didn't know was that by 2013 our life would be taking such a seismic shift that I'd never fill them in again.

By 2016 when those forms dropped through the letterbox for my youngest child, they were firmly filed in the bin. And then a few months later a reminder also made its way to the bin. By the third and final, very aggressive reminder I was on the phone to the admissions department of our local authority. Not because I had suddenly seen the error of my ways, but to ask why they would be so bold to assume I had forgotten, given that I'm a parent of four children, three of whom had been through the process but were now all home educated. I genuinely find it fascinating that they were able to seek us out to send these forms through health services but were seemingly incapable of connecting the dots between their department and the home ed department across the corridor. Go figure.

## Confession time

I didn't want to be a home educator. There, I said it. You see, we came to home education via the school backing us into such a corner that they effectively off rolled (but not quite) my then six-year-old child. Five years previously I had given up a job I had loved to stay home and look after my medically unwell child and while I of course didn't regret that, I wanted my life back. I wanted to go back to work and drop my smiling kids off at school and not see them until I picked them up from the after-school club. I wanted to just trust the school staff and teachers to do what was right for my children and have them deal with the challenges. I was not what I would consider 'home ed' material and so when we were forced to deregister, I was angry. As far as I was concerned, school was where kids were supposed to be and I was supposed to get to be someone other than mum, once they went to school! I saw other parents drop and go on the school run and I was just overcome with how unfair it all was.

However, once I began to process my grief and anger at a system that let us down, I began to learn about the children I actually had in front of me, instead of the children I expected to have. I worked on letting go of the fantasy 'perfect' family I had created in my mind. And while it was hard coming into home ed when it wasn't a positive choice, it did get better. I mean it must have, otherwise I wouldn't have deregistered the other two and refused to send the youngest! Now, years down the road I'm instead angry that I didn't know I could do this as a first choice instead! The realities of home education have far exceeded any pretend life I thought I wanted but it took time, a lot of unlearning and gentle, compassionate care with myself. It was a process. But it's not the same for everyone. It's also okay if you never fall in love with home education. It's okay if this never becomes the way of life you didn't know you needed. Just as school can be a means to an end, so can home ed, so like me, if you have also come to home education through anything other than a positive choice, please know you are not alone, and it really is okay and entirely normal to feel all the emotions.

Please take each day as it comes, however it needs to look and most importantly be gentle with you and your children while you adjust. Confession over, let's get back to it.

## A brief history of home education law

Alas, we don't know what we don't know, and I certainly didn't know back in 2007 or even in 2011 some really super important facts about education in England, that I wish I had. Back then, I didn't know I had a choice. I thought I had to send my children to school. It never crossed my mind to not apply for school as surely that would get me in trouble with authorities as once your child reaches a certain age, they have to go to school right? School is compulsory. Plus, I didn't want anything different to the status quo anyway.

It's fair to say that the school is compulsory programme worked well and continues to do so even in 2023, based on how home education is still a hugely misunderstood educational option. The government simply omits the facts and leaves it to parents to seek out information they don't know they need to know and so, the myth of school being compulsory holds firm. Forms arrive, parents aren't aware school is optional and round we go, so let's get clear on the information I didn't have, so that you do. Education is compulsory, school is not.

First up - parental duties. It's actually parents that are responsible for ensuring their child receives an education, not the state. In England our most recent education act is the Education Act 1996 and in section 7 it states:

*7. Duty of parents to secure education of children of compulsory school age.*

*The parent of every child of compulsory school age shall cause him to receive efficient full-time education suitable -*

*(a)to his age, ability, and aptitude, and*

*(b)to any special educational needs he may have, either by regular attendance at school or otherwise.*

What that little piece of legislation tells us is that we are responsible for ensuring our children are provided with an education and that as parents, we can discharge our duty either by sending them to school or otherwise. Otherwise means, by making other arrangements of which home education is one. (Spoiler - Home Education is of equal legal standing to school too simply via those magical words 'or otherwise') We actually have some of the best rights in the world regarding home education and even with the government pushing towards deeper oversight, we remain one of the only countries where home education is something we are entitled to do.

This leads us beautifully to number two, the default education in England. The default education in England is, have you guessed yet? Yes, it's Home Education. Mind...blown! (Well, my mind was, when I discovered this) Education is the duty of the parent to secure and all educational avenues except for home education require an active opt in. Private school - opt in, state school - opt in, academies - opt in. If you simply do not opt into an educational service, ta da! You are by default, home educators.

This is because state schools are a governmental service. This service is provided for those who want and need it and the government is required to provide a space at a state school to any child who wishes to make use of it. But, and here's the important part - you don't have to. As the parent with the duty to secure an education for your child, it is your choice how you fulfil that duty. Those school application forms are simply invitations providing one of your options in case you've opted not to home educate. How's that for a reframe?

Something that is often misunderstood is the reality of who home educators are. Once upon a time most parents in the country would have provided their own children's basic education, as schooling was for the rich. Church schools came to be, and then State schools, with laws formed around compulsory education, so that over time, it became standard and compulsory for children to receive education in a school. By the late 1800's many children were attending some kind of schooling, but this was costly, and many working-class families could not afford to send their children, as well as needing their children working to help support the family too. By the early 1900's school fees (other than private schools) had been abolished and attendance increased, however there were those from the upper classes who chose to continue to provide the education themselves privately with tutors, governesses or private church led education. By the 1940's, this option extended down to the upper middle classes, again via private tutors.

Understandably this led to a general assumption that anything other than school was for the upper classes only and this myth still remains in 2023.

In truth, nowadays home educators come from all walks of life and home educate for all manner of reasons. Home educators come from every religion, every ethnicity, every family type, every socioeconomic background, and geographical area and this is regardless of their individual education level, income, or social connections. So, what changed?

One thing that changed in 1944 was that the Butler Education Act was passed, introducing a legal duty for parents to ensure that each child be educated according to their individual aptitude and ability either by regular attendance at school, or otherwise and in 1954 a middle-class mother, Joy Baker began home educating her children as per the 'or otherwise' clause in the Butler Education Act. This caused quite the stir as the original intention of the 'otherwise' clause had been to ensure upper class and upper middle-class families were able to continue educating at home via private tutoring and it hadn't occurred to the government that ordinary people would even consider making use of the clause for themselves! Joy Baker fought her Local Authority for 10 long years, facing numerous court appearances, fines, possible prison sentences and even having her children temporarily removed from her care, but on 15th November 1961 she finally won the legal right to educate her children at home when she managed to convince the courts that her interpretation of 'or otherwise' was accurate and applied to all, regardless of social class.

The battle that Joy Baker fought gained widespread publicity across all 10 years and beyond, paving the way for many in the middle classes to become aware of this possibility for themselves and with the launch of the internet in the 1990's home education gained further momentum and popularity moving downwards into the working classes too. With families able to access more information and support than ever before, home educated children now represent just under 1% of all compulsory school age children. We have gone from there being as little as 20 known home educating families during Joy Baker's time, to around 10,000 by 1995 and approx. 100,300 today! (Educational Freedom FOI July 2023)

*The legalities of home education and deregistration.*

So, you're considering home education but you've no idea where to even start. In terms of the legalities, home education is of equal legal standing to a school education meaning not only is it legal, you do not require anyone's consent to do it either. This applies to all children equally including those children with special educational needs. Becoming home educated in England is a simple process but can require a little more work depending on your circumstances. I've included the usual circumstances below to give an idea of what I mean. Please note I am referring to England only as education across the UK is devolved and so Wales, N. Ireland and Scotland have differing rules and guidelines. If your child has never been registered at a school, you can simply continue as you are and you will become home educators by default. There is no need or obligation to inform the local authority of your decision and you do not need to register as a home educator.

If your child is registered in a mainstream school in England (with or without an EHCP) and you choose to home educate, you can simply provide a letter of deregistration to the head teacher. It's a very simple letter stating the correct legislation that applies and that should be it. Deregistration essentially means informing the school that your child will now be receiving an education otherwise than at school and this then triggers the school to remove your child's name from the admissions register and inform the local authority of this change.

If your child is registered at a special school, you need to seek consent. This consent is not to home educate, but to remove your child from the school roll (for any reason).

If you are separated from the child's other parent, it's important to remember that parental responsibility applies equally unless there are specific court orders in place and therefore both parents should agree around educational decisions where possible. This isn't always the case of course and it only requires one person with parental responsibility to deregister, just as it only requires one to apply to school. The most sensible route is to discuss home education with the other parent where possible. In general, local authorities will have an understanding that the parent with whom the child lives for most of the time, is normally in effective control of the education provided and whether the child attends school and the parent who does not agree with home education would have an opportunity to apply to the courts if they are unhappy, however its best if parents can reach an agreeable view on what is in their child's best interests.

It is more common than you would expect for schools to have very little knowledge around home education or the legalities of it and so some schools will not know the correct process to follow or may even suggest it is not as simple as deregistering. Put simply, they're wrong and I would always advise that you refer troublesome schools to the law on education (Education Act 1996) and the regulations around admissions/ deletions via The Education (Pupil Regulations) (England) Regulations 2006.

You are not obligated to discuss your thoughts with anyone while considering home ed, to justify or explain your decision, give reasons, or attend meetings and this is especially true after sending a deregistration letter as it is a legal instruction applicable without delay, but it can sometimes be helpful to provide information to ensure that your reasons are properly recorded for home education data.

Whether you 'chose' home education as a first choice, came to it via philosophical choice or came to home education via negative reasons, you are in good company. There are as many reasons for home education as there are home educators and although there is a trend in home education rising due to school system failures, it doesn't mean there needs to be an issue or that you won't come to enjoy and love the life you didn't know you and your children needed regardless!

*Time for a breather and a quiz!*

That was a lot wasn't it! Well done for getting this far. Learning about home education can sometimes feel like a full-time job in itself, let alone the actual doing of the home education! Later we will get acquainted and cosy with how home ed happens in all its various styles but for now, make yourself a cuppa, maybe grab some cake and do a little dance. Just to check you've taken the info in, have fun with a little end of chapter quiz! (Groan)

What is the official term for home ed?

Who is responsible for ensuring children receive an education?

What is the main factor contributing to children's unhappiness right now?

What kinds of people can home educate?

When was the Butler Education Act passed?

Who was Joy Baker?

What percentage of school age children are home educated in 2023?

## Reflection

Think about your reasons for considering home education and reflect on where you sit within the 'choosing' to home ed space right now. (Wherever you are be kind and gentle with you)

# The Local Authority

It wouldn't be a home education book without a chapter about the Local Authority so I'm including it early on. This is so we can get through it and then focus more on home education itself rather than the governmental oversight of it. When I first became a home educator, governmental oversight wasn't a big thing at all in most areas of the country and it's frankly crazy how quickly the lay of the land can shift. In the time I've been a home educator, local authorities' powers have moved to a place of far greater oversight. The England guidelines that I began home ed under, stated very clearly that the statutory guidance relating to children not receiving an education did not apply to home educators. This concept probably sounds alien to many home educators reading this as you've likely been educating under the 2019 guidelines since you started but it really was a thing. Ah, the good old days!

*EHE guidelines 2007 - 2023*

Local authority guidelines in 2007 stated that home education was not within the scope of making arrangements to establish the identities of children who are not receiving an education yet in 2019 the guidelines changed to state the opposite. How did we get there? Let's have a look.

*"2.6 Local authorities have a statutory duty under section 436A of the Education Act 1996, inserted by the Education*

*and Inspections Act 2006, to make arrangements to enable them to establish the identities, so far as it is possible to do so, of children in their area who are not receiving a suitable education. The duty applies in relation to children of compulsory school age who are not on a school roll, and who are not receiving a suitable education otherwise than being at school (for example, at home, privately, or in alternative provision). The guidance issued makes it clear that the duty does not apply to children who are being educated at home."*

Our Government (regardless of who is in charge) has had a significant bee in its bonnet around home education for the last 20 years and many events between 2003 and 2010 came to a head after local authorities were promised new powers to monitor home education with a 'light touch' only to find the new guidance stated the opposite and that the new children missing education statutory duties did not directly apply to home educators or give LAs additional powers.

In January 2009 it was announced that Graham Badman would be in charge of an inquiry into home education and then came the dreaded Badman report of May 2009. Do look it up if you want to better understand the history of how we got to where we are. All of the recommendations in his report were accepted in principle without inquiry and home education looked set to become highly monitored across the country under the guise of safeguarding and to protect children from forced marriage and domestic abuse.
Thankfully after much back and forth with lobbying from home education communities, Lords who value educational

freedom, select committee inquiries into the legitimacy of the Badman report, but mainly, a general election, Graham Badman's recommendations never went forward. In April 2010 it was announced that the proposed home education licensing scheme had been scrapped and with it a new coalition government came to power shortly after. Hooray!

Alas this was not the end but instead a mere intermission, a brief calm before the next storm that of course came in the form of yet more education select committee inquiries, reports and members bills from grumpy Lords. In 2012 the select committee launched a new inquiry into home education focusing on improving 'support' to home educators. One of its recommendations was that the Department of Education review their guidance surrounding home education. In 2018 consultation regarding new guidelines was sought and the new guidelines came out in 2019. The biggest change being that home educators were now in the scope of the children missing education statutory duties. The complete opposite of that which was stated in the 2007 guidelines.

Then in 2020 the select committee launched another round with recommendations in 2021 for a statutory registration scheme, higher monitoring of home education with insistence on seeing children, seeing 'work', and regulating literacy and numeracy similar to that which we see in schools via SATs. The children not in school consultation was launched culminating in the school's bill in May 2022. This bill aimed to place a legal duty on parents to register under a CNIS (children not in school) register. This bill was dropped in Dec 2022. In June 2023 Flick Drummond MP introduced a private members Bill under the 10-minute rule bill to push for compulsory registration of home educators and in 2023 the government sought a way round this by instead attempting to amend regulations regarding children with EHCPs and those on child services plans to make it more difficult for them to deregister. This kind of legislation amendment does not require the same scrutiny as a new law and so can in theory, be easier to do. At the time of writing this book, those measures have not been brought in. There are many more examples of the mission push towards regulation and monitoring of home education, but these are the basic footnotes.

The reason you need to know this is because local authorities have duties and powers in relation to children who are not receiving an education, and since 2019 this has changed to state that home educators are in scope of this duty until the local authority receives information regarding the child's education. Because of this it is important to know how it all works.

## Local authority behaviour

Some LAs are great and some are awful, there is no getting away from that. I've supported other home edders in the general community for years and the extent to which some local authorities overstep the law is genuinely shocking. When I say some LAs are great, what I mean is that they do the job that is expected of them, while being respectful to home educators. They understand the law and apply it appropriately.

What a family might expect local authority contact to look like, often clashes with the realities of dealing with them, sometimes in wonderful ways and sometimes, horrendous ones. You might have heard horror stories and so expect awful things, only to be relieved at how well your LA behaves. You might be expecting a supportive, kind, helpful LA worker only to find instead an overbearing school at home type of bias being pushed on you. What's even more annoying is that it's not even about specific LAs. It could be just one staff member in the team, when the others are lovely or one lovely one who then moves on. It's just all so unpredictable and changeable. On the plus side, the reason it's changeable is because the guidelines and laws are ambiguous and allow interpretation on both sides of the coin. By both sides, I mean that home edders are just as entitled to interpret the guidelines in their own ways too. Because of this, finding common ground where an LA works *with* the home ed community and vice versa is essential and many LAs do so.

Despite home education being of equal legal status to a school education, the government's view is that the best place for education is in school and this view filters down heavily into local government meaning many staff responsible for home education inquiries have biases and conditioned views of what they feel education should look like. I personally live in a reasonably well-behaved local authority. As a home ed community we work hard to maintain strong relationships with the EHE team at the LA, so that they are able to extinguish their duties and we are able to home educate with minimal interference. Sadly, not all LA'S behave in this way, regardless of community endeavours which is why understanding their duties and your responsibilities is essential.

A local authority (LA) or local government is a subsection of the government who are responsible for various local services such as social care, housing, transport, and education in your area along with neighbourhood services. There are currently 317 of them in England but only 153 are responsible for education. To make it extra confusing there are different types of LA within all of that too and only some are responsible for children's services in your area. Some are county councils, some are district councils, then we have metropolitan districts, London boroughs and unitary authorities.

There are two types of structure, tier one, and tier two. Tier, one structures are unitary authorities, London boroughs and metropolitan districts. This means that all services are provided by one local government. Tier two structures are made up of a county council that is then then separated down into district, borough, or city councils. This means that services are split between both the county council and the district, borough, or city council. You may even live in an area where this is further split down into parish or town councils too. Now you are suitably confused, you may be pondering why I am giving a lesson of the governmental structure of England and what it has to do with home education. While ultimately it is parents, not the state, who are responsible for ensuring children receive an education, the government also has a duty towards the general welfare, safeguarding and education of all children in the country. This duty falls to the local authority to uphold.

Previously this was held under the local education authority (LEA) to distinguish which authorities held a responsibility regarding education, but when The Children's Act 2004 was introduced, education and social care were combined causing a restructuring that left the term LEA obsolete. Nowadays education falls under general children's services via the LA instead, which frankly does little to help with the confusion of who your LA for Home ed is.

One example of this is Hampshire in the South of England. Hampshire is a county council local authority that then has several districts and boroughs within it. For the majority of home educating families, their LA will indeed be Hampshire. But those living in Southampton, Portsmouth or Isle of Wight are not under Hampshire as these are unitary authorities and provide all services themselves. All of this to say that the council who you pay council tax to or who organises your bin collections is not necessarily the council who is responsible for education in the area.

There is no available way to make the next bit more fun or interesting. I'm sorry, I have tried but sadly some things really are just boring but necessary. Each LA has various responsibilities and duties around children and education but the ones most relevant to home education are:

s.436a The Education Act 1996

s.437(1) The Education Act 1996

s.439 The Education Act 1996

s.438(2) The Education Act 1996

## s.436a identifying children not receiving an education

s.436a places a duty on the LA to make arrangements to identify children who are compulsory school age but are not receiving education.

*A local authority must make arrangements to enable them to establish (so far as it is possible to do so) the identities of children in their area who are of compulsory school age but*

*are not registered pupils at a school, and*

*are not receiving suitable education otherwise than at a school.*

This is the main duty that LAs contact home educating families under. Their basis for this is that until the LA is aware that a home educated child is receiving a suitable education in line with s.7 of The Education Act, these children may be in the scope of this duty (commonly referred to as children missing education or CME). Because of this, LAs are able to contact home educating families via informal inquiries to ask about the education being provided to and received by the child. There is no legal obligation for families to respond to informal inquiries but it's sensible, so that the LA can confirm that your child is not in the scope of their duties. Often if an LA has concerns after receiving information, they will come back to the parent and ask for additional information. This is preferable to more formal procedures and the best use of their time; however, they also have additional duties they can discharge if this does not provide them with what they require.

## s.437(1) Notice to Satisfy and School Attendance Orders

If the LA does not receive information to confirm a child is not within the scope of their duty, they are able to serve an order known as a notice to satisfy or NTS. If they still do not receive information that satisfies them, they can serve a school attendance order or SAO.

s.437(1) states that:

*If it appears to a local authority that a child of compulsory school age in their area is not receiving suitable education, either by regular attendance at school or otherwise, they shall serve a notice in writing on the parent requiring him to satisfy them within the period specified in the notice that the child is receiving such education.*

*That period shall not be less than 15 days beginning with the day on which the notice is served.*

A notice to satisfy (NTS) is a formal legal notice from the LA that requires you to satisfy them within 15 days that your child is receiving a suitable education. Up until this point there is no legal requirement to satisfy the LA but as above, it's sensible to respond to the LAs informal inquiries so that there is no need for things to become more formal.

*If (a)a parent on whom a notice has been served under subsection (1) fails to satisfy the local education authority, within the period specified in the notice, that the child is receiving suitable education, and (b) in the opinion of the authority it is expedient that the child should attend school,*

*The authority shall serve on the parent an order (referred to in this Act as a "school attendance order"), in such form as may be prescribed, requiring him to cause the child to become a registered pupil at a school named in the order.*

If the LA is still not satisfied after serving a notice to satisfy, they can issue a school attendance order. However, the LA must follow a specific pathway for school attendance orders. They should first make informal inquiries, ask for more information if required, issue a notice to satisfy then await a response. If they remain unsatisfied, they should consult with schools before then serving a notice of their decision to the school before writing to the parents of their intention to issue a school attendance order, naming the school on the letter of intention. Once a school attendance order is issued it will have the name of that school on the order and state that the LA requires the parent to cause the child to become registered at the school named on the order. The relevant sections of the Education Act 1996 are s.439 and s.438(2).

## s.439 Consulting the school

*(5) Before deciding to specify a particular maintained school in a notice under section 438(2) a local authority shall consult*

*(a) the governing body, and*

*(b) if another local authority are responsible for determining the arrangements for the admission of pupils to the school, that authority*

*(6) Where a local authority decide to specify a particular maintained school in a notice under section 438(2), they shall, before serving the notice, serve notice in writing of their decision on*

*(a) the governing body and head teacher of the school*

## s.438(2) Notice of intention to serve the order

This section relates to the notice of intention to serve the order that the LA must follow. Again, they must follow the proper procedure otherwise they will need to start it all again. This is why boring stuff is necessary to know.

*(2) Before serving the order the authority shall serve on the parent a notice in writing-*

*a ) informing him of their intention to serve the order,*

*b) specifying the school which the authority intend to name in the order and, if they think fit, one or more other schools which they regard as suitable alternatives*

It's important to recognise that SAOs are not commonplace. For the majority of home educators, informal inquiries are all that is required to confirm the education. It's also important to note that not all SAOs are issued due to the child not actually receiving an education. Some LAs have a history of requesting unreasonable information from parents and exerting far more oversight than the law allows, and this can lead to them issuing SAOs based on parents not providing information the LA wants but isn't necessarily entitled to.

Their behaviour should always be reasonable and proportionate.

If an SAO is issued, the child is not automatically registered at a school. Only persons with parental responsibility can enrol children in a school. It therefore becomes the parents' choice to comply with the SAO and register the child, or not. If the parents choose to comply, this is effectively agreeing that the child was not receiving a suitable education and it is right that they be enrolled in school. SAO's that are complied with remain in place for the length of compulsory school age, unless the SAO is revoked by the LA. Again, boring but super important to know.

Parents who choose not to comply with the SAO by registering the child, may then be prosecuted. This enables the parent to go to magistrate's court and argue their defence. The defence against an SAO is to evidence that the child is in fact, receiving a suitable education to the judge. The judge will weigh up the information available and make a decision. If they decide the child is receiving a suitable education the SAO will be quashed and you go back to home educating as usual. If they decide the child is not receiving a suitable education the SAO will be upheld and the parent will be convicted. Conviction for failing to adhere to an SAO has a few options but most commonly these are a financial fine. The SAO is then discharged as conviction has happened and the process would need to start again with the LA requesting information or the parent deciding to register the child in school.

Importantly this still does not mean the child is registered at a school unless the parent enrols them. It remains the parents' responsibility to do so. Convictions around SAOs can result in the LA applying for other orders such as an education supervision order or a parenting order. Education supervision orders can allow the LA to enrol children without the parents' approval.

All of this is why knowing and understanding the laws and guidelines around home education is so important. Currently, everything starts with the LAs ability to make informal inquiries based on their statutory duty to identify children not receiving an education and so when looking at LA contact, this is the basis home educators need to approach from. Their duty is a reactive one. They are not there to tell you what a good job they've decided you are doing or to approve of the education you are providing. They are not there to monitor the education or tell you what you should or shouldn't be doing. They don't even need to agree with how you are home educating at all. Their entire job is to check that the education objectively meets the legal requirements of section 7 of the education act 1996; being full time, efficient and suitable to that child. They must work to the same laws and guidelines that parents do. The LAs duty is to children who are not receiving an education. So, when they make informal inquiries and you provide information, it's to confirm that your child is not within their remit. If after their inquiries they feel your child may not be receiving a suitable education, their job is to step in and use all those yucky bits of the law because their duty is reactive around children, they discover may not be receiving an education.

And that is why this chapter, while law heavy and snore worthy, is so important.

## Providing information

You've become a home educator; your family are slowly starting to deschool and find your feet and suddenly you've received a letter from the local authority. They are introducing themselves and asking for a little information on your provision and so naturally, you break into a sweat and panic. Firstly, find solace in the fact they sent you a letter because that is good behaviour from a local authority. Some local authorities do horrendous things like knock on your door without warning or constantly call you.

**Side note** - Do you remember back in the day when someone wanted you for something, they came and knocked your door? You would open the door to see who it was and then have a chat on the doorstep or invite them in. Or opening the door was how you then arranged a time to meet up for a catch up instead? Kids would knock on the door to see if little Jimmy could come out to play. Ah the good old days! Well, mostly those days are gone. Technology has changed how we interact with each other and nowadays someone knocks the door, and we think 'oh my gawd, who is that!?' While ducking behind the sofa and turning out the lights. That's because we now have letters and email and phones and texts and WhatsApp. I don't know about you, but my friends now text me to let me know they are gonna call me, let alone the idea that they might show up at the door unannounced! Unfortunately, some local authority workers seem to have forgotten that we've moved on from knocking doors. They seem to have forgotten that they can send a letter or email and they don't seem to realise that in 2023 humans don't even answer their phone unless they know who's calling, let alone answering the door to a stranger! So, for those of you who do happen to have local authorities that have not yet entered the 21st century, here are my handy tips for dealing with them if they knock on the door unannounced or call you.

### Do.

Do feel free to ignore the door.

Do feel free to not answer the phone.

Do feel free to refuse to discuss personal information on the doorstep.

Do feel free to refuse to give details over the phone.

Do feel free to refuse to let an LA worker into your home, announced.

Do feel free to tell the LA to email or write instead of calling.

Do feel free to remind the LA of the EHE guidelines.

Do feel free to assert your right to respect for your family life and  privacy

### Do not.

Do not shout f*** off through the letterbox.

Do not answer the phone and shout f*** off down the phone.

Do not answer the door and throw water in said person's face.

Do not shout to an imaginary child 'Emmett get back in your cage'.

Do not let an aggressive dog chase an LA worker off your property.

Do not tell the LA that you think the government monitors your calls.

Do not tell the LA that their laws do not apply to you because you are under maritime law.

Do not open the door with a rifle in hand to assert respect for your family life and privacy. (Even if you are a licenced gun user)

Okay. Now that's covered, let's get back to the more reasonable well behaved LAs. Remember, LA staff have a responsibility to children who are not receiving an education. They are simply people doing a job just like anyone else and so by providing information, you are confirming that your child is not their remit. You can do this in a range of ways. You could have a call with them, meet with them for a chat either at home or in another location, or provide them with a report on the education being provided. What's important to understand is that you are able to choose how to provide the information. Some LAs may suggest a call or visit would be best, or they may even pre-emptively book a visit date and time. You do not have to agree to that if you don't feel that is best for your family. The wording of informal inquiries will often have a bias towards the way the LA would prefer to work and show them attempting to assert authority, when actually this is a partnership. You are the one responsible for your child's education and they are responsible for children who are not receiving an education, so while yes, it is sensible to provide them with information, that doesn't mean you need to bow to their every whim. Keeping the LA within their remit is essential.

So, what do they need to know? They need to know about the education your child has been receiving and how that objectively meets the responsibilities laid out in section 7 (Ed Act 96). They do not need to know what education might take place in the future as their remit is around identifying children not receiving an education at the time they make the informal inquiry, not children who may not receive an education in the future. Remember, they have a reactive duty, not a proactive one.

What I wish I knew about LAs before becoming home ed is that they all approach their duties in vastly differing ways and so generally, your local home education community is the best place to gain an understanding of how your LA behaves and how you then would like to deal with their inquiries. Many national home education support groups are fantastic and worth their weight in gold for the support they provide families having issues with their local authority, but this can also be a double-edged sword as taking generalised national advice can backfire especially as each LA works differently. One example I've seen is families taking national advice despite the local community advising the opposite which then caused the local authority to change their approach to the community, increasing demands for more detailed information when they were previously happy with less. I've also seen it go the other way too, with a LA being overbearing and this being corrected through national support. Basically, local first, national if needed.

As a general rule, most LAs just want to extinguish their duty in whatever way is easiest for them and while you don't have to adhere to what's easiest for them if it oversteps the law or EHE guidelines, it is sensible to provide them with information on your child from an education perspective, their way of learning, how you meet any special educational needs they may have, the content of the education being provided and how you ensure they have social opportunities. LAs do also have a natural focus on numeracy and literacy as these are super important for being able to live in and contribute to society when grown. As long as you are covering these things in the information provided, most LAs will be satisfied that your child is not their remit. I'm not going to go into the specifics of how you may want to do that as it's important that any information you provide to the LA is in a way that best represents you and your family and there are also lots of support groups out there for those that do need a hand.

In conclusion, yes, the LA will probably contact you at some point as they have a duty towards children who are not receiving an education. They tend to contact families annually, but some don't and may leave it longer. Providing information to them that shows your child is not their remit is the most sensible option. It is a partnership with the LA, not a dictatorship and the EHE guidelines lay out what is and isn't expected of the parent and of the LA. Being confident in the law and the EHE guidelines is essential to ensure you are able to communicate well with the LA and keep them to their job, while you do the busy one of home educating your children.

*Time for a breather!*

Learning about legal stuff is always brain numbing so do get some fresh air, coffee, wine, whichever is most appropriate for you!

And it's of course time for a reflection.

Do some research into your local authority.

What is their local policy around home education? How does that match up with the EHE guidelines for LAs 2019? (Or the most recent guidelines if this has changed)

What is the local home ed community experience of your local authority?

How does this match up with the LAs local policy and the EHE guidelines for LAs?

What are your feelings around engaging with the local authority?

What are your fears and worries? And most importantly, are they valid based on all of the above research you have gathered?

Being well informed and confident in your responsibilities and the LAs role is an essential part of being a home educator and while you may see horror stories in national groups, knowing the current situation in your local area is where you can find your own way forward.

# Deschooling and Education

Okay let's get into the juicy stuff. Welcome to home education! Whether you chose this as a first choice or as a result of deregistration from the school system, the work begins now. Spoiler - By work I don't mean setting your child up at the table with pen and paper. (Although you certainly can if you want to, just read this chapter first) Your first lesson as a now fully fledged home educator is actually to learn about deschooling. Something worth mentioning straight away is that the whole time you are deschooling, you are still home educating. There is often a misconception that deschooling is a space in which no learning happens. This could not be further from the truth, but as you read on, you'll come to understand that it's just a very different sort of education. It's probably a good time to warn you that this chapter is a beast so take it piece by piece and come back to it regularly!

Deschooling is a social philosophy developed by Ivan Illich. Ivan was an Austrian Priest, Theoligist, philosopher and social critic who wrote several books relating to his ideas around institutions and the damage they can cause. His now famous book: 'Deschooling Society' published in 1971 is often cited in connection to deschooling as a principle part of home education.

*'A good educational system should have three purposes: it should provide all who want to learn with access to available*

*resources at any time in their lives; empower all who want to share what they know, to find those who want to learn it from them; and, finally, furnish all who want to present an issue to the public with the opportunity to make their challenge known'. Ivan Illich 'Deschooling Society' 1971*

Illich's main argument was that the institutionalisation of education (and other services) has created needs and problems that they had originally sought to solve. As a result of this, it has generated complete dependency on school as education and caused us to defer to the authority of school-based systems as the experts on anything education based. This has led to a belief in our society that those in the school system authority are the only people or institutions able to provide education.

When we look at the history of schools and home education in a previous chapter, we can see that schools have quickly become institutions for education. The word school has become synonymous with education. When I tell you to think of a large animal with big ears and a long trunk you think of an elephant right? When I tell you to think of education, I'll bet you immediately think of school! (If you didn't, well done, I bow to your deinstitutionalized greatness) Basically schools have become the centralised and accepted organisation in which we in our society believe people can,  and do receive an education and we've been 'schooled' or conditioned to believe this as a fact, even though it's not because, Spoiler - education is nothing to do with school as an institution and in the context of home education, understanding this and applying it, is exactly what deschooling is all about.

As new home edders explore this exciting and probably terrifying world of home education it can be hard to know where to start. Many new home educators start by following the National Curriculum (institutional programme of school) or doing subject lessons. I know I did and for many this makes total sense because we start with what we already know, but when we commit to reflection on our own education and conditioned ideas around what education is, we find some really beautiful ways to do this thing called home ed that might have you throwing the ol' NC in the bin!

## Confession time

I always thought I loved school. There were of course funny little stories of how the teacher would have to drag me off my mum's leg in reception class, or that time I kicked a certain someone in a delicate area for lifting up my skirt in primary school and I was the one sent to the head teacher. There was also of course the extra help I got for maths because no matter how hard I tried, it just wouldn't go in. But I loved seeing my friends and I loved art class and music class and my word I loved the productions we put on in uppers. I can still remember the words and actions to so many of the amazing songs our music teacher had composed.

By secondary school I was well established as creative and over sensitive, rather than academic. A child who could do well if only she would apply herself and stop allowing her passion for justice and her sensitivities to cloud her focus. Then, life got complicated at 13 and I went from an A's and B's student (except in maths) to being predicted ungraded. I applied myself in one or two classes (History and English being my favourites) and spent most of the rest of my time angry, anxious, and rebellious. I remember at 14 we had to stand up in history and give a talk about an inspirational speaker in history. This kid here? I chose to speak about Adolf Hitler. My talk was inspiring. It was deep and compelling and educated and thoughtful and had I been speaking to a group of adults such as lecturers or teachers, it probably would have gone down really well! Instead, it was the cause of an all-out riot in the history department from fellow 14-year-olds unable to conceive of the idea that Hitler could be both a horrendous human being and also a bloody fantastic public speaker. For my fellow peers (by school-based standards) it was not possible to separate fact from emotion and that talk earned me some nicknames I won't repeat here. Essentially, teenhood was tough. Tougher than for most and so I did what all good irresponsible young people do and rebelled in spectacular fashion. The theme album of my teens was Jagged Little Pill played full blast on repeat...enough said. I became ill at 15, struggling to complete my exams but came out of school with all of them, gaining a respectable selection of B's and C's and the expected D in maths of course and a repeated quote from both teachers and family of 'imagine how well you could have done if...'

By 16 I couldn't think of anything worse than carrying on in school institutions and I didn't. That little girl who was so full of inquiry and wonder and excitement about the world, had been replaced by someone desperate to escape anything that might look like learning. Yet I still loved to draw and dance and sing. I worked in jobs where I had to learn new and interesting skills. I found creative ways of solving problems and I researched everything within an inch of its life. I generally became the go to person in whichever job or office I was working in at the time. As an adult, I still love to read and write and research. I still love to draw and paint. I still love singing and dancing, and I still hate maths, despite being pretty good with numeracy.

On reflection, did I love school? No, but I think I loved the idea I was sold about it. I was sold the idea that school was where I went to get all my deep burning questions about the world and humans and life answered. School was where I would finally understand how things work. And it's that super salesmanship that caused me to put my own children into the same system I went through too, despite it all. Thankfully of course, I'm here writing this book having home educated four children at various points and currently watching a never been to school home educated nine-year-old learn about steam, who is still full of the awe and wonder and inquiry that I lost long before his age. Confession over, let's get back...

This is the thing with home education. However, you come into it, it will cause you to reflect a lot. It will cause you to pick apart your own school experiences and take you on your own learning journey you never imagined going on. It will cause you to unlearn so much of what you thought you knew about education. Also, what no one tells you about becoming a home educator is that with time, you will become a leading expert on child development, approaches to learning, individualised learning and learning styles, the state of the current education system and the politics that guide it, and quite possibly become proficient in the art of educational and SEND law if you are really lucky.

As you use all of this newfound learning and unlearning, your approach to home education will go through several changes. There'll be times you feel you know exactly what you are doing, and others you'll feel up stream without a paddle wondering where that weird smell is coming from. Did I mention that words that you didn't even know existed will become commonplace in your vocabulary and that you won't even bat an eyelid about it? Let me know when it happens to you!

But through it all, through this beautiful, wonderful messy experience, you will come to understand something really important. You'll come to understand that learning and education has very little to do with school and that it's actually a lifelong pursuit that you aren't getting out of and hopefully one that your children will not want to escape from any time soon.

## So, what actually is deschooling?

Deschooling is a word used by the home-ed community to describe the adjustment period that parents and children experience after a child becomes home educated, it happens alongside any learning and is also ongoing learning in and of itself. It's a practice of reflection, unpicking and reconnecting the dots, across your learning journey. It's not a quick thing and I am still deschooling as a regular practice 10 years on. There is an often-cited suggestion that for children, deschooling should take place for one month per year that the child has been in school, which while lovely as an idea, is not really that helpful in reality. This is because I don't feel deschooling is an accurate term to represent the child's adjustment journey into home ed and it also leads to incorrect assumptions that no education is taking place while deschooling. Instead, I would encourage parents to view their child's journey as one of decompression and adjustment. When we apply deschooling principles to children it muddies the waters between deschooling and decompression and can inadvertently project the responsibility of unlearning onto the child. Children need time to decompress and adjust and they need a parent who is able to model deschooling to them.

When we think of decompression most of us would think of altitude but for home-ed children it is the reduction of pressure around them as they adjust to a new and different environment. It's the process of relaxing into home education and finding equilibrium again. Sounds weird when the new and different environment is their own home, and therefore is just home right? But it's not. Home has suddenly become the thing that has replaced school in simplistic terms and psychologically this has an impact. When parents commit to a practice of deschooling this helps guide how easily that decompression and adjustment can happen for the child.

The reason I suggest this alternative view is because having been active in the home ed community for a number of years, I've found that actually, children rarely require deschooling. They are generally pretty honest and upfront about what doesn't work about school system mindsets and practices, and they continue to be very honest and upfront about that when they become home educated too! Children's behaviour is communication, and they resist the things that we parents try to implement, if and when it doesn't suit their learning style. In fact, it is this resistance and behaviour from our children that is often the perfect starting place for our own deschooling as parents.

For parents, deschooling is about adjusting to an utterly different way of life and unlearning what we've been 'schooled' to believe about education, as well as relearning what education actually is. As said above, it's an ongoing process and is also not just for parents of children who have been to school. Even when your children have never been to school, like the large majority of us, you probably have and therefore will try to implement systems that make the most sense to you, based on what you were taught. The beauty of most children is they will tell you why that doesn't work for them pretty quickly! Deschooling is about us reflecting on our understanding and conditioning of education and then learning to let go of what doesn't work for our children, so we can move forward into what does.

*What does decompression look like for children?*

When we think about why our children may need a period of decompression and adjustment, we only need to look at the typical school day.

- Children in school have a strict structure that dictates their days from wake up to bedtime.

- They have instructional, teacher-led learning.

- All of their time during the day is scheduled by someone else.

- They spend a surprisingly small percentage of their time with parents.

- They have very little autonomy.

- They are essentially told what to do, what to learn, how to learn it and when.

- Motivation is also often extrinsic, either to gain reward and praise or to avoid criticism and punishment.

This is without the more complex potentials of children coming to home education with trauma, school-based anxiety, mental health struggles and or disabilities.

Those first few months of home ed can be amazing! And they can also be really hard. They will probably be both. If you followed the pathway that's become standard in England, you've likely had your child in some kind of setting outside of the home since they were tiny. Nursery, childminder, play school or preschool, reception class, infant school, primary, Upper, secondary/high school. Children who follow this pathway often spend as much as 6-9 hours outside of the home each weekday. You will have spent periods of time together that look different to that - namely school holidays and weekends. But essentially, you and more importantly, your child has been in a system of instruction since they were small, and those instructive environments have clear impacts on how your child behaves. For parents whose children struggled in school, you may be familiar with the daily morning and afternoon/ evening meltdowns or the difficulty of holidays and how much your child requires of you during these times.

Depending on how long your children have been on this pathway can also be suggestive of how much decompression may be needed, but not always. Typically, the longer a child has been on the school pathway, the more challenging it will be for them and you to decompress and deschool. But for some children, as little as 6 months in the school system can cause trauma that requires a trauma informed approach, for life. Deregistration doesn't magically fix that and it's a major adjustment for all of you. Your child is used to interacting with you for a minimal amount of time each day, and vice versa. Meltdowns might lessen, or they might increase due to the change. You might find that your child requires even more of you in those first months, or they may just want to sleep and spend time alone. During decompression your child will be going through so many adjustments and while they may welcome not having to go somewhere they found hard or difficult or traumatising or boring, the transition to home can also leave them feeling lost, confused, angry or low. You've always just been mum/dad/caregiver and now suddenly you are also the educator. It might be that it all feels such a relief to deregister that it all starts amazingly and then as the weeks go on, things start to lose momentum, interests dwindle, heads start butting. If you were brought up in the pathway that's become standard, it's all you've ever known and all your child has ever known and that's a lot to unpack, which takes time. By time I mean weeks, months, sometimes years, but none of that means it wasn't the right choice or that you've made a mistake and none of that means you aren't both doing the absolute best you can with the situations you are experiencing.

Home ed is by its nature, a very different way of life in comparison to the typical school experience. Even if you follow a strict structure and school at home set up, it's still different and so autonomy and the ability to say no is a really common first expression of decompression in newly home-ed children. As the parent you probably have all these wonderful timetables and plans lined up. You are excited to get stuck in with this learning 'thing' and along skips your wonderful child. You ask if they are ready to start their day of learning but instead of jumping in enthusiastically, the first thing they do with this newfound learning freedom is to say 'Nope. Not doing it!'. And while it probably feels frustrating and worrying for you, that release of pressure your child has initially experienced will lead to some really interesting places for them and for you, if you allow their decompression to happen.

## So where does deschooling come in?

Deschooling comes in alongside your child's decompression and adjustments and alongside any education that is happening. It's the work that we as parents do so that we can allow home-ed to have the best possible chance of working well. For that to happen we have to start with our own recognition of what we perceive education to be. I'm going to be super honest here. If you think you and your child are the exception to the rule and don't need to deschool I'd recommend cosying in close for a firm but loving reality slap. I've been you; I was wrong and so are you. Those of us who need to deschool the most are the ones that do it the least. Do you know why? I believe it's a combination of guilt, panic, and the cognitive dissonance that deschooling presents. In deschooling, we are faced with new information that conflicts with existing information and beliefs we hold, leading to confusion and stress and so we do what most humans do, we avoid the thing causing the stress. Except it doesn't work, because without deschooling, the stress to come is far harder to cope with in the long term.

This is why deschooling is the work and why some of us shy away from it, especially when everything already feels so hard and challenging. School based mindsets seep into everything and it's natural for that to happen because school is an institution in our lives and has been for a good few generation. My first child went to school in 2007, I went to school around 1987. My dad went to school around 1960, my gran went to school around 1928 and it's likely my great granny went to school in the early 1900's. That's 5 generations of school-based mindsets and systems that have changed a lot less than you would expect. As I'm talking about my Scottish dad's side of the family, we could actually go all the way back to 1696 when Scotland became the first country to make national education compulsory.

**Side note:** This wasn't as wonderful as you may think as one of its primary aims was to ensure everyone received a specific education with a goal of wiping out Gaelic. By the time the 1872 education act came in, Gaelic was fully repressed, and students punished physically for speaking the language. This is how easily we can become institutionalised into a belief that education has to happen in a specific way. The school-based mindsets around Gaelic was that it was wrong and must be corrected and stamped out to be replaced with English. This was seen as a marker that the 'education' of Scotland had been achieved.

When you look at just my timeline of school on my Scottish side, you can see that only 7 generations back my ancestors' primary language slowly disappeared and by the time it got to my gran, no Gaelic was passed on at all. Understandably my dad didn't know a word of Gaelic and so I've been learning it third hand and via no native speaker, slowly and with varying success for years.

**Extra side note:** This is also a prime example of how education can be efficient (does what it sets out to do) but completely unsuitable (for the Scottish people).

## School-based mindsets

I've mentioned school-based mindsets several times now so let's chat a bit more about what I mean and why I feel it's important to reflect on them. School based mindsets are all of the tiny little unconscious mindsets we've picked up our own school system pathway. They are the beliefs we've been schooled into and the associated emotions we feel when we discover conflicting information about them. Let's cover 2 of the more common school-based mindsets below.

**You must go to school to get an education.**

I think this one is the most ingrained and the one that drives other mindsets too. Our society views education as a commodity. Children receive this raw material of education so that they may become the finished product and become a commodity of society, valued, and accepted for what they bring into the economy. (Sorry, was that a little cynical?)

*Reflection- What does the word education mean to you right now?*

Society uses school to socialise us into the mould of the society around us. That's literally one of its jobs and why the school system continues to model the factory set ups of the industrial age. Our particular societal model goes a little like this: Go to school, work hard, make friends, get good grades, pass exams, get a job. (Optional add on here of: go to college, go to university, get a degree) get a job, fall in love, get a mortgage, get married, get a bigger mortgage, buy a hire purchase car, have kids, work harder to afford all the stuff, see less of your kids and spend most of your money on childcare for the children until they go to school and then spend the next 12 years working to give your children the best educational chances, so they can do exactly the same as you. Do not pass go, do not collect £200. The societal expectation is that you go to school, get an education and everything else will work out from there and when you do, you'll be a full-fledged, valuable, and contributing member of society. The main issue with this internally running belief of course, is that it is an absolute fabrication or, utter bollocks as my husband would say.

When considering the actual subject matter of this belief (education) we have to reflect on what education actually means to us when we take school out of the equation. In terms of definitions of education, the most common is 'the transmission of knowledge and skills' but I personally love the definition that education is simply 'purposeful activity to achieve specific aims'. Such a generalised and flowery definition really allows freedom for education to define itself and so naturally appeals to my autonomous approach to it! Contrary to what we've been schooled to believe, there are actually lots of different kinds of education with most falling between two main types: formal and informal. The school system is one type of education and is classed as formal education. Almost all formal education takes place in some kind of institution with specific aims and goals defined by those in charge of society.

Education is also sometimes defined by its approach such as teacher led, child led, self-directed, or by its origins such as Charlotte Mason, Montessori, unschooling. Basically, education comes in many forms and school is only one of those.

Assessing our beliefs around the actual word is important too as it can also allow us to distinguish education from indoctrination. Education as a word is rooted in the Latin words "educare", "educere" and "educantum" all of which vary slightly in meaning, but essentially as they are all connected, they are taken to mean that the aim is to provide a child with a nourishing environment to bring out and develop the potential of said child. I don't know about you, but the more I dive into unpicking this unconscious mindset around education and school, the less it seems to be talking about school, at least as we know it today.

Unpicking our belief that you have to go to school to get an education doesn't mean that the aim of education nor the societal expectations, no longer apply of course, but it enables us to consciously choose how we want to educate our specific children, what it's aims are for them and how we choose to partner them to be a part of the society that they will exist in.

The indoctrination of a school-based education fits us neatly into the model where most of us come off the conveyor belt to become employees to large corporations rather than employers, small business owners, inventors, or creators. Instead of contributing to society with what we are good at, we come to an acceptance that we have a specific place in society that we cannot step outside of. Yet the government's aim for education is that it does not prevent your child from reaching any goal they so choose. It's all at odds with itself and I don't know about you, but I want my children to be cogs in a machine they value, that feels purposeful and that they are proud to contribute to, no matter what type of cog they turn out to be.

**Activities are either educational or non-educational.**

This one is not true in any circumstance, yet school-based mindsets trick us into believing it anyway! For example, our conditioning tells us that education only happens between 8.30am and 3pm with a uniform on, in a classroom, with a teacher at the front and children sitting still, being educated by said teacher. When a child is unwell or late, schools delight in informing us how many hours of learning have been 'lost'.

*Reflection - what does learning mean to you right now?*

And that infamous quote from school institutions everywhere, provides us with a segway into another important word that needs an introduction, Learning! If education is the act of providing a nourishing environment to bring out and develop potential in a child Then, to learn, is to acquire knowledge or an ability to do something. Alternatively, to learn could also be to attend a course or other educational activity or to gain knowledge from experience so as to improve or to simply come to know; to become informed of; to find out a thing. I like to think of education in a really abstract way and that helps to not get stuck in school-based mindsets and comparisons. For me, education is the act of providing the environment for the child, learning is the act of supporting the child to acquire knowledge or ability and wisdom, is stepping back so they can work out what to do with it. The idea that some activities are educational, and others are not requiring us to again, unpick our own thoughts and understanding of what learning is when we take away school. It requires us to reflect on why we view some activities as educationally valuable and others not and why we are placing that value judgement on the activities of our children.

In school, we are taught that learning is a structured linear program with specific boundaries around it. The national curriculum is one such linear structure. Learning is separated out firstly into age related cohorts, then into classes, with the day separated into specific subjects, with stages for each of these subjects but in reality, life is not separated into neat little boxes, and neither is learning. Firstly, humans are experiential social animals and learn best when in a rich environment that provides an assortment of people from all ages and experiences. School is the only environment in our lives, in which humans are sorted into cohorts according to an age range. Secondly, the idea that learning can be actually separated into subjects is hilarious. Almost everything we do is a mishmash of skills building on other skills. Baking a cake is literacy, numeracy, and science but we'd never get a cake made if we were told we had to do it as an English test only, the cake would suddenly become theoretical and abstract without the physical chemical reactions and numerical measurements of ingredients. Learning is everywhere all at once and refuses to be pigeonholed, even if we are taught to believe it can. And lastly, learning is not linear. It's messy and abstract and tangible and repeating and complex and beautiful! So much more beautiful than any of us have been schooled to believe.

*Time for a breather and an activity!*

Again, that was a lot, and we only explored the nuance of deschooling and 2 potential school-based mindsets you may have! Let's take a breather, have a cuppa, and do a little celebratory dance. Put this book down for a bit and allow yourself to process. When you're ready, come back and do the below activity.

**Socratic questioning activity.**

Have a think about the following questions and write down your answers.

What is the reason you decided to home educate?

What was it about home education that made you choose it?

Or maybe it's about school, what was it about the way schools work that made you choose home ed?

What do you want home education to achieve for your child?

We are social animals and learn from the traditions and stories and social rules that exist around us. One of the stories that has become prevalent in our unwritten social handbook over recent generations, is around school and education, as we discovered in the above chapter. But here's the thing. Just because you have a philosophy about what you think education should look like, or have begun deschooling, doesn't mean societal conditioning won't keep trying to play its part. The trick is to catch yourself doing something and ask yourself why. Take the example of educational worksheets or workbooks. You could ask yourself:

Why am I printing these off? Who am I doing this for? What might happen if I don't give the children worksheets or workbooks to do?

Write these questions down and then listen to the answers you give yourself. Write those down too.

For each response, ask yourself "Do I really believe that?" And then: "Why?"

You might go round several times with this. Write it all down. Write down all the thoughts that pop up from simply stopping to ask yourself why you are doing the thing. This is a wonderful way of seeing the internal dialogue you are genuinely experiencing around the things that you may or may not want in your home education.

I can guarantee you'll be amazed what comes back from such simple internal questioning! This form of Socratic questioning is super beneficial if you want to better catch your old school mindsets and clear them away, so that you can focus on what you truly believe and act on it,  whatever that is.

Give it a go!

# Home education styles

As humans we really do love a label to describe the stuff we do and what we are. We say we don't and that labels are restrictive but there is no getting away from the fact that they make it easier for ourselves and for others. We already wear lots of different labelled hats throughout our day. For me some of those are: mum, wife, sister, daughter, friend, home educator, autistic person, disabled person, woman, unemployed and unschooler.

Each label has a subtle (and sometimes not so subtle) difference in how we are seen, how we act and how we interact, with some labels being connected to others and some being standalone. If I say I'm an unemployed, autistic, disabled woman this gives a very specific description that others will interpret in various ways. When I say I'm an autistic, unschooling home educator, this again gives an entirely different perspective. I am all of those things and so much more in-between, but labels can help us to find people who understand us, they can help us to get the support we need and that can also enable judgements too.

Being able to say which style of home education we connect with, can help us to find our people and help us to feel safe. So, I get our need to classify ourselves and set up camp *somewhere*. I only wish I had known that the actual doing of home education matters far more than the style it aligns to. I spent many a deep dive and rabbit hole exploring different home ed styles when I could have just been diving into connection with my children and seeing where that takes us. With that said, let's have a rambling wander around the concept of home ed styles and then explore some of the common ones because labels, they help us humans.

Firstly, it is worth noting that it takes time to develop a home educating style and the first step to this is recognising that the overall home ed style needs to suit the child receiving it. I know that sounds obvious, but you'd be surprised how many of us will lean towards styles that don't actually suit our child. The style also needs to suit the family as a whole of course, but this must be a secondary consideration for good reason. The majority of us parents have been through the school system and therefore have our own bias, conditioning, and blocks around what learning can and 'should' look like. Styles that are more formal and structured are naturally more appealing to many of us, even when we are acutely aware that they didn't work well for us or potentially even our child. It's just that they follow a path more closely aligned to a school education and therefore they feel safer and less risky, especially when you are newly deregistered and finding your feet in a brand-new world! As you are introduced to all the other ways in which people can learn that can feel freeing but also overwhelming! How will you know how to do it right? What if you destroy the children's future by picking the wrong style?

Thankfully there is a simple hack for this: Focus on your child. Becoming observationally focused and letting your child lead, allows you to consider how your child learns, how they interact with their environment, and how they move around activities and interests. This is the gold dust of home education and ensures you are actually settling into a rhythm of learning that is genuinely suited and individualised to the child in front of you. By approaching home ed in this way, you take the pressure off of you and get to allow your child to tell you what they need from you instead. All of this is not to say that your thoughts, views, experience, and guidance isn't valuable. It's super important that as home ed parents, we find ways to make life work for everyone, including ourselves, but we can do this without sacrificing our child's preferences if we simply put that first instead of last. When we home educate our children, we have a unique opportunity to provide them with respect, trust, and autonomy in their learning, which is rarely received anywhere else so why wouldn't we start there!

### Structured, Unstructured, Autonomous

Secondly, when considering your home ed style it's important to know that there isn't one style that is better than another and each has their merits. For me, all of the various concepts and buzz words we will explore below, actually fall under two main categories with a third acting as a holder for all approaches that are solely directed by the child. The two main categories are structured and unstructured with the third 'holder' being autonomous.

**Structured** home ed is a formal approach to learning, with opportunities provided via a predefined framework of outcomes. It is structured according to a plan, either externally chosen from existing frameworks or created as you go along.

**Unstructured** home ed is an informal approach to learning with opportunities provided via a flexible and responsive mix of approaches or content, that is framed by the child's interests and skills without a predefined outcome in mind.

Many parents misunderstand **autonomous** home ed as being informal and unstructured, but it can be formal or informal depending on where the child chooses to take their learning. The opportunities are discovered by the child in a self-directed fashion, via their inbuilt intrinsic motivation for problem solving, with the child then constructing their own solutions, ideas, and knowledge from their discoveries. An autonomous child may direct their own learning towards a plan of study with a specific outcome, which would be a structured autonomous approach, or they may direct their own learning towards informal methods without a specific outcome in mind which would be an unstructured autonomous approach. The main difference in whether the home ed is autonomous or not, is in who the motivations have come from. Autonomous education is always solely directed by the intrinsic motivations of the child, regardless of the method chosen by them. This is then facilitated by the parent.

As the parent, you may approach home ed from a structured style but  allow autonomy in how the child completes the tasks. 'Allow autonomy' is a bit of an oxymoron in itself as autonomy is the act of self-governance. Would the power dynamics of a parent choosing to 'allow' autonomy in certain things mean that it's not really autonomous? That's one for you to ponder.

**Routines, rhythms, and patterns** exist within structured, unstructured, and autonomous approaches too but are separate to the learning approaches themselves. Autonomous and unstructured home edders can, and often will have routines and rhythms to their days, weeks, and months with patterns of learning becoming recognisable through different individually chosen markers such as seasons for example. Structured home edders can and sometimes do have no routine or rhythm to their days, weeks, or months other than ensuring planned study is completed on a predefined timescale. What is clear though, is that all approaches involve present, connected, and motivated parents who have their child's best interests at heart and are aiming to provide the best outcomes for their individual child in question.

*Common Home ed styles.*

Let's explore some of the more common styles of home education in England. These are my own views of them and as you develop your own understanding, you may see them with totally different definitions, which is exactly as it should be. There are many home education styles and approaches and the beauty of home ed is that you don't have to pick just one forever. You don't need to have the next sixteen years all figured out, nor do you need to necessarily have a pre-defined specific goal in mind for the education but what the education should do is to enable the person receiving it, to participate meaningfully and independently in society by the time they are adults, without blocking them from any avenues they may wish to venture into. Right, let's explore.

## School at home

This is a classroom style set up that usually looks very similar to school. Educators may choose to refer to themselves as homeschoolers rather than home educators. There is often a structured curriculum, timetable, a start and finish time with structured breaks and the education tends to be instructional, with the parent filling the role of the teacher. Some families have a uniform, school name, mottos and desks, chalk/white board and a dedicated homeschool room. Lessons are typically separated into academic subject areas and the style often mirrors the style and content of education in schools but with the benefit of one-to-one teaching and less disruption.

## Structured /formal

Structured education is sometimes confused with school at home, but they can often be very different. A structured style often comprises timetables covering specific areas of learning deemed important, with lessons then delivered by the parent or an outside resource such as tutors, online schools, online classes, in person classes or learning centres. Following the National Curriculum is common, but some families also follow other curriculums or make their own. The general setup is often more relaxed than school at home, as the main focus is on ensuring the learning happens, rather than on the room, clothing, or way the learning is presented. Structured education can also be autonomous if the child is the one leading the structure, lesson plans etc. This approach often follows a routine that separates learning into different academics or topics, but it can also work as a cross curricular approach via topic-based projects.

## Semi structured

Semi structured educators often approach the education as part instruction-led and part self-directed, but this is a very varied style and open to many definitions. It can look like specified lessons for one part of the day and then following interests for another. It can look like specific academics covered each week for a predetermined amount of time. Some semi structured educators use tutors or online lessons for subjects they feel are most important and then allow self-directed education at other times. It can also look like following a curriculum or plan but with an alternative curriculum. Many semis structured educators appear to split their day into formal learning and non-formal learning but do not necessarily place more importance on one over the other.

## Project based or PBL.

Project based learning or PBL is a hands-on interactive layered approach that is often cross curricular. Project based learning is an approach of studying a particular area of interest over a longer period of time and will often contain many areas of learning and be multi-layered to include various subjects. This style often centres around a problem or challenge to solve but can also centre around a particular interest in general. It can look like the school-based theme of topic work. For example, 'The Romans' as a topic will weave through many lessons and subjects over a period of time. In home education this can look like a child raising a question or noticing an issue they feel needs solutions. It can also look like a child developing a special interest in an area of learning such as 'dinosaurs' 'lego' 'reptiles' or a specific time period or culture. Instead of separating into subjects, learning is via projects with each one providing a rich level of learning in many areas over a longer period of time. Projects often include diversions and expansions into other areas that become relevant as the project goes on too.

## Unschooling / free style / self-directed

These are all synonyms of the same style and feature a philosophy that children should be trusted to lead their own learning journey, with them directing their education in whichever way they feel is most important and effective for them. Learning is often seen as a part of everyday life and there is no separation or segmentation. This often feeds into a whole life and parenting approach rather than only education and many follow a collaborative, non-coercive respectful style of parenting and living. This style can include any and all other styles of home education as long as it is being directed by the child rather than the parent. Parents facilitate and partner children in their education rather than directing or instructing and children are trusted that they will learn what they need when the skills are required by them.

## Eclectic

Eclectic home educators mix and match a range of styles, approaches, and resources to provide a highly individualised education to each child. It bases the focus on the child and what their strengths, styles and interests are to develop an education that may include elements of many different approaches.

## Tidal / Seasonal

This style recognises that learning happens differently at different times and encourages the freedom to adopt different styles and methods at different times. This can sometimes be connected to the seasons of the year, or the seasons of development seen in the child. It can also flow in and out of varying pathways and approaches in a rhythm that the family come to recognise as cyclical. It recognises that learning will have ebbs and flow but that it is still happening regardless. Families may follow a more structured approach at certain points and a more unschooling approach at others or it may be that formal learning happens in the colder months, with hands-on outdoor learning happening in warmer months.

## Gameschooling

Gameschooling is a form of play-based learning in which board games, interactive computer games and card games are used in an intentional way as a main or partial basis for the child's learning. Some gameschoolers focus solely on tabletop gaming, i.e., board and card games and do not incorporate computer or video games in their home education provision and others do it the opposite way round. Gameschooling can also be used as part of any other Home Ed style.

**World schooling**

Worldschooling is a philosophy that encourages children to learn from the world around them and usually involves international travel. There are lots of ways to do it with some families travelling nonstop, and others worldschooling from a base, renting out their house while they travel. Some may travel only part-time, and some may not even travel at all but use the travel-based adventures of others as a foundation for their learning activities. Worldschooling can be a part of an overall style or may form the entire provision, but the emphasis is on immersion in global experiences to learn.

**Montessori / Charlotte Mason / Steiner / Classical/ Religious based education**

These are specific methods, theories and styles of education that can be followed rigidly, or elements used to form part of the education. There are specific movements for each of the methods and many carry their own curriculums to follow.

*Confession time*

When I realised, I would have to home educate, I had visions of colour coded timetables, curriculum aims and happy enthusiastic children sitting at the table waiting for some world class learning to be taught to them, by me...Oh what a bumpy ride I was in for! Not only did I envisage these things, but I also actually tried them too. After all, autistic kids thrive on routine and clear aims and objectives, right?! What I came to learn, thanks to my kids, is that I not only had a lot to learn about education, but I also had a lot to learn about neurodivergent brains because it turns out my kids do not thrive on routine at all and neither do I. Instead, routine was the only way they could get through the day in a world designed for neurotypical people. Routine was a self-regulation tool, designed to help them deal with the unknowns around the corners and as soon as they felt safe and secure to say no, they pushed back against these routines and timetables immensely and I was left floundering in a world that I felt I was failing as a mum and home educator. Then someone suggested unschooling. I jumped in and read all the books and as I learnt more about it, I realised it made absolute sense to me. After all, As an adult, when I'm directing my own experiences and co-creating with others, I feel purposeful, focused and in the zone! I feel respected and appreciated and valued. Why would I not want us all to feel like that in our family? So, I began the slow and ever-present practice of unpicking what I knew about education, learning, development, and parenting. Because of this my kids learn every day and so do I. They have free choice in what they learn, they have free choice in what they try and don't try, and they have free choice in how they do that. My role has moved from that of a parent and teacher to one of their student and partner. I spend a lot of my time watching them learning and understanding what they are learning. I spend a lot of my time chatting, expanding, debating, and discussing with them. I spend a lot of my time looking for ways that I can better facilitate what they are learning and exploring, and I continue to spend a big chunk of my time unpicking all the stuff I learnt previously! Don't misunderstand, these kids are not left to their own devices languishing, they simply direct themselves and my job has become about helping to get them where they plan on going.

As a home educator, I'm not against planning, scheduling, or timetabled plans. We use a loose weekly timetable to ensure we attend the events and groups the children enjoy. I'm not against academics or structured learning and if my children wanted that, I'd provide it. I'm just against doing those things when they don't work well for my child. I'm against doing them just because everyone else seems to do it that way.

I'm against doing them because that seems to be what others would approve of more easily and I'm especially against knowing none of it works well for my clan but doing it anyway because I think I should.

The whole point of home education is that it opens our children up to possibilities, rather than restricts them and so whatever your home ed style, do it because it's what is right for the child you have in front of you. Okay, back to it!

*Education Philosophy*

Developing your educational philosophy is something that tends to happen over time as you find a rhythm and try various approaches to work out what fits well for your child and family. An educational philosophy is basically a statement that identifies and clarifies your aims, beliefs, and values in relation to your child's education.

The law says that the parent of every child of compulsory school age shall cause him to receive efficient full-time education suitable to his age, ability, and aptitude, and to any special educational needs he may have, either by regular attendance at school or otherwise.

But what does that mean? Let's break it down.

Parents = persons with parental responsibility for the child.

Child of compulsory school age = term after 5th birthday to last Friday of June in the academic year that they turn 16.

Obligated = legally responsible for

Cause to receive = make sure the child is given and receives the education

Efficient = achieves what it is intended to achieve

Full time = occupies a significant proportion of the child's time

Education = system of learning

Suitable= appropriate for the person and enable them to participate fully in life when an adult

Age = Appropriate for the person's age

Ability =  person's own skills (and for education-allows progress for that person's skills)

Aptitude = natural ability

Special educational needs = learning difficulties or disabilities.

An important part of the suitability of education is laid out in guidelines via the use of previous case law.

The EHE guidelines for LAs 2019 states that "*The term suitable should be seen in the following light: It should enable a child to participate fully in life in the UK by including sufficient secular education. This means that even if the home education is primarily designed to equip a child for life within a smaller community within this country, it should not foreclose the child's options in later life to adopt some other mode of living, and to be capable of living on an autonomous basis so far as he or she chooses to do so. This view is compatible with the small amount of potentially relevant case law*".

So, to summarise, as parents we are responsible for making sure our child is given and receives a system of learning that is appropriate to their age, skills, and natural abilities, while considering any learning difficulties or disabilities. This system of learning needs to enable them to fully participate in life as an adult and occupy a significant proportion of their time, while achieving what it sets out to achieve.

When we look at the legal goal of education laid out in this way, we can see that it's actually open to interpretation and this is necessary, to ensure that all children are able to receive the education they need, rather than just an education in general. This also enables us to begin forming how we want to achieve the goal.

Remember, academic subjects are not a requirement for home education but confidence and ability in literacy and numeracy is of course essential. After all, these are the foundational skills used every day, out in the world by all of us. The suitability of education is that it enables a child to participate in society fully and they need numeracy and literacy for that.

This doesn't mean you must follow a specific curriculum or method of formal study, as there are many ways to develop these skills, with most of them occurring naturally via living life and experiencing things that show a need for the skills. In time, this more informal learning sometimes develops towards exams, to show ability and enable moving forward into other study but again, there are a wide range of options available.

Nearly 10 years on, I'm pretty clear and confident in my educational philosophy. For me, the goal of home education is to help my children to explore who they are and to create an environment where they can expand into who they are becoming with learning happening naturally as a side effect of that. In our home, there is no separation or labelling of what is and isn't learning. There is just life, and we learn naturally as we live because I believe the only thing children really need help with, is how to access the information they are seeking and then interact with the experience they are having. I believe children avoid learning only when it's something they don't have a need or desire at that time to learn about and when children are trusted to direct their own learning, given the freedom to choose their experiences they will learn what they need and more, from it. Yes, my children spend their time doing things I don't enjoy, but I can sit with them in the joy they experience and facilitate them to enjoy it even more because mostly, I believe the more happy, engaged, and enjoyable something is, the more we naturally learn from it, including hard things that are challenging. When we are supported through challenging and hard things it can bring us to a place of seeing frustration as a beautiful tool for growth. I believe that freedom to choose is where the intrinsic motivation to learn comes from. We are born with it and then instructed out of it. So, my goal is to support these humans in my care, to discover and explore life every day in their own ways, knowing and trusting that in doing so, they are learning more than I could ever hope to teach.

Earlier in this chapter I said that there is no particular style that is better than another, but do you know what the best kind of home education is? It's the one that suits your family, the one that puts your child's learning first, the one that recognises learning can happen in many ways. It's the one that accepts that school is just one way to be provided with an education and It's the kind of education that seeks to find all the ways that might suit the learner you have in front of you! Tailor your home education to the child in front of you, the family you have and the needs that exist in your family.

School is a package deal. If you opt into it, you opt into all of it. But what we often fail to remember is that Home ed is a package deal too.

If you opt for the default education in England, you opt into all of it. You opt into the freedom of choice, and the overwhelm that comes with it, you opt into not having someone else plan the learning for you, you opt into learning about educational theories and styles you didn't even know existed and you opt into being with your children for amounts of time you never thought you would. You opt into what feels like the scariest DIY project you ever thought possible.

So, whether it's schedules, structured, unstructured or a bit of everything, as long as it allows you the freedom you need to find your way as a family that is exactly what you should be doing. It may well stay that way too if that's what's best for your child.

*Time for a breather and an activity!*

To assist in developing my own educational philosophy and to help establish my confidence as a home educator I had to unpick lots of my own conditioning around learning and education, but I wish I had someone who could have provided me with some starter questions on that journey, so here are some for you! Take a look at them and write the first thing that comes to mind. Then, reflect on your answers and dig a little deeper.

What are my goals for home education, and do they match my child's goals for their own journey?

Do I separate play and learning?

Do I believe children won't learn something unless they are taught?

Do I believe children naturally avoid learning?

Do I believe children can be trusted to direct their own learning?

Do I respect the choices my children make in how they spend their time?

Do I value some forms of activity over others? Do my children and do those match?

Now go and celebrate with cake. I highly recommend it!

# Self-directed learning and unschooling.

You might think I'm showing bias by doing a chapter on self-directed learning considering I've already included a chapter on home education styles in general, and you would be absolutely correct. I am passionate about autonomous, self-directed learning and the beauty that it can bring to your life as a family so hold onto your hats because an info dump is incoming.

I always think of my second youngest when I talk about self-directed learning. He was only on the school-based pathway for a few years and yet nearly ten years on, he still struggles with difficulties and challenges around the genuine trauma he experienced. He was a very unwell baby and so spent a large majority of his early years in and out of hospital. I had given up work when he was one as no nurseries would take him, due to insurance risk and he had attended preschool sporadically due to illness and overall concerns about meeting his needs when there. Before starting school, I had requested he be kept back until the following year as a summer born baby and also due to his complex needs and was refused. We requested a statement, but we were refused. We requested more support, but we were refused. Even when well, he was still required to go to hospital regularly for lots of tests which were three-day visits to London, plus emergency care at the local hospital as and when. His attendance at school was always low and by year

2 was significantly low. He had many delays, regressions and significant speech difficulties and had always had a lot of distress around going into school, but school is the best place for kids, right? I didn't know at the time there were any other options. I was constantly bombarded with attendance processes, complaints, and threats. I requested an EHCP. I was refused. Then, the school decided to refer him to CAMHS. CAMHS assessed quickly and thoroughly and discovered that this tiny little complex kiddo was severely anxious while in school. In their assessments they got him to draw pictures of his family. I was nowhere in the pictures, and I can't even tell you the panic I felt! But then, the lovely psychologist explained that I wasn't in the pictures because this 6-year-old currently had a younger than average emotional and social understanding. He did not yet understand that mummy was separate from him and so every time I left him at school, he was literally missing a part of him, and it was causing him significant mental and emotional distress! He was also diagnosed with a working diagnosis of significant autistic traits. By now this 6-year-old showed signs of trauma, had severe school-based anxiety, self-harm, medically complex needs and had just been diagnosed with autistic traits with significant speech, social, emotional, and behavioural delay. We went back to the school with the findings and again, requested an EHCP. We were refused. We requested support. We were refused. We requested he be moved down into year 1. We were refused. We were eventually backed into a corner, and I had no choice but to deregister. But guess what? That severely unwell 6-year-old? Is now a strong, healthy 15-year-old with stable medical needs, his anxiety is barely an issue, he's

bright, inquisitive, funny, engaging, kind and above all he is happy and thriving and do you know what else? Everything we've done since the early days has been autonomous and self-directed. Guess what else? This approach is not without considerable work.

I also remember I felt guilty that I waited so long before deregistering my eldest child, at 11 years old, but mainly I felt panicked and worried as home educating a primary age child is completely different to home educating a secondary age child. I struggled to deschool around this, so I looked at some beliefs and conditioning I had around it. The below word salad is how just one round of internal dialogue went.

*'The real work starts at secondary school. So, primary age children are okay to play and have fun learning, but secondary age children have to do 'work'. But hang on, they are only 11. Only 6 months ago they were primary age. How can it change that quickly? Also, I know home-ed teens who don't do anything that looks like work, and they are doing amazingly? How does that work then? Maybe they are just the exception. What do I mean by work anyway? I mean putting pen to paper at a table and studying something. I need to download some worksheets and then I'll feel better about it all. At least we'll have done something then. Hang on, said 11-year-old child didn't ever put pen to paper in school anyway, so does that mean they were doing nothing there? No, of course not because a teacher was teaching them! Ah, so I need to teach them then. But I'm not a teacher? Arghhhhhhhhh...I know, let's print something off written by a teacher!'*

Does any of that sound familiar? At that point my brain failed to reconcile the conflict and reverted back to a school-based mindset as that's what was more comfortable. I then interrupted said child's wonderful and valuable learning experience so I could make them do a worksheet to make me feel better, because well, they are of secondary age after all, right? And this my friends, was 6 months into my deschooling journey. It really is a life's work. Phew, I don't know about you but I'm tired just reading that, let alone constantly going through it, but it's definitely worth it.

What we know about child development shows a very different picture in terms of children's learning. Child development tells us that learning is the lifelong process of acquiring knowledge, skills and information and we do this from birth. It's the child's interplay between who they are developing into as a person and their direct environment. But it's more than that, from a purely physical perspective we know that young children's hands take a significant amount of time to develop into being able to accommodate fine motor skills. The hand skeletal structure is not finely developed until between 6-8 years old and while of course lots of intricate fine motor skill play helps with the development of skills, there are many things that a 3- or 4-year-olds hand is just not supposed to be capable of doing, until later due to the simple fact that it takes time to develop the structures, dexterity, and coordination. Despite this, children in the UK begin school earlier and earlier and with it come expectations such as dressing and undressing independently, managing their own toileting, managing zips and buttons and hair bands, holding pencils and writing.

To demonstrate how ridiculous it all is, here are a few expectations of early learning goals from the national curriculum for reception class, which means these are 4- and 5-year-olds.

*Fine Motor Skills:*

*Children at the expected level of development will: - Hold a pencil effectively in preparation for fluent writing – using the tripod grip in almost all cases; - Use a range of small tools, including scissors, paint brushes and cutlery; - Begin to show accuracy and care when drawing.*

*Writing:*

*Children at the expected level of development will: - Write recognisable letters, most of which are correctly formed; - Spell words by identifying sounds in them and representing the sounds with a letter or letters; - Write simple phrases and sentences that can be read by others.*

*Managing self:*

*Manage their own basic hygiene and personal needs, including dressing, going to the toilet, and understanding the importance of healthy food choices.*

These are early years foundation learning goals, birth to five and while yes, some children will manage this, many more will not. This won't be because there is anything wrong, but simply because they weren't ready yet. It doesn't mean they aren't learning; it doesn't mean they are behind. It's because these school-based expectations aren't what learning is. It's what the goals of the school system are.

## Bloom's Taxonomy of learning

There are lots of theories and models put forward about how we learn, and each have their merits. But one of my favourites is Bloom's Taxonomy of learning. Instead of seeing the output of learning as the acquiring of a skill, it sees the learning as a mental and psychological process. In this model children with a rich environment acquire knowledge pulled from the environment and then go through a variety of stages, to embed that into a system they can then apply to situations.

The model follows a pyramid approach with knowledge at the base and evaluation at the tip. In this model knowledge is the foundation upon which learning is built and we then explore developing new skills from that knowledge base.

- Knowledge in this model is about being able to remember or recall facts, information, procedures.

- Built upon that is comprehension which is simply being able to understand and interpret that knowledge.

- Next is application which is using what you've learnt from the knowledge and comprehension and applying it to new situations or to solve particular problems.

- Then we move into analysis- Being able to pick out particular parts of the knowledge because you understand and can apply the concepts to other things.

- Into Synthesis- which is combining elements of everything above into a new idea, procedure etc.

- And finally, evaluation- assessing and judging the value of the learning in particular situations.

To show this in action, let's make a cup of tea.

- Knowledge is recalling the instructions of how to make tea.

- Comprehension is understanding why you make tea in that way and interpret that info into an action i.e.: making the tea.

- Application is applying this to making knowledge and comprehension in a different way. For example, you don't have a kettle, so working out you can still make tea, using a pan to boil the water instead.

- Analysis is using what you learnt about tea, to try making coffee and applying parts of the tea making process to that and understanding you add coffee instead of a tea bag.

- Synthesis is combining your new skills of tea and coffee making and applying them to a new skill like cooking a food that needs boiling water and ingredients added to make the food.

- Evaluation is recognising that anyone who makes tea by putting the milk in first, hasn't understood the assignment.

It's a silly example (except for the evaluation because I'm serious) but when applied to the concept of learning, we open ourselves up to labelling much more activity as learning than we first thought and helps us to see that learning is not the subjects of English and maths and geography and science. It is the interplay between a person and the environment they are in, and what they then do with that and are supported to do with that to grow and develop. It's why all activities are educational. All activities provide a rich and fascinating learning journey for the learner but we as parents run the risk of dismissing that beautiful learning, if we continue to put our own school-based values on those experiences.

There is often a misconception that unschooling or self-directed learning is lazy, permissive, or neglectful parenting. It would be a really short chapter if I just said the misconceptions are wrong and left it at that, so let's have a deeper look. The term permissive, along with authoritative and authoritarian, were coined by clinical and developmental psychologist Diana Baumrind back in the 1960s with neglectful being added by later researchers. Despite our understanding of parenting and education moving on significantly since these terms were coined, they continue to be widely used, with authoritative parenting receiving the most positive bias, so understanding them can be beneficial and is especially useful when home educating.

For many families the parenting style and view of children in general will inform the way in which you approach home education. It may even have had a part to play in why parents might move towards home ed in the first place, but if your children went to school, you will have been taught how you are expected to support the structures and systems of school-based learning regardless of your parenting style. You see, you've been schooled to see education and parenting as two distinct and separate things, with education being the thing that happens via someone else such as a teacher, and parenting being the thing that happens the rest of the time. This is an easy view to take when your children are not in your company for the majority of their perceived educational input, but not quite so easy when both education and parenting are happening in the same space and time, all the time.

In truth parents are a child's first educators and that looks nothing like teaching. For the first few years of a child's life, it is through their parent's love, care, attention, and encouragement that children grow and develop. It is through the act of interaction, connection and support that children try and eventually take on skills. Children are like sponges, taking on information and forming meaning from it at astounding rates and surprisingly they don't need instructions in how to do it, it's just kind of hardwired. Have you ever tried instructing a toddler in how to walk? Or instructing a baby on how to talk? I'm giggling at the thought! They pick up these skills via interactions between themselves and their environment, with the people they trust most in the world, their parents, or caregivers. Parents and caregivers play one of the most important roles in a child's development and I find it really sad that not only has the importance of this been slowly degraded over time, but that the idea of parents as educators has been essentially decimated in favour of separating parents from their children for early enrolment into the school system.

Let me be clear, this is everything to do with our government and society and nothing to do with what is best for children and their development. It's important to remember that different models of the schooling system exist all over the world and there are many that do respect the role of caregiving, upbringing, and parents in a child's education. The German model is one such example (despite home education being illegal) and the Finnish model is another. In these examples, early education is seen as the first and most critical stage of lifelong learning. Early childhood and education is viewed as a cooperative journey between parents and society with a more formal education not beginning until children are older.

We know that parental input is such an important part of a child's first years, with the majority of a young child's brain development happening in those early years before school age. We know this development commonly happens under the care and connection of parents, family, and the child's close community. We know children who develop deep trusting relationships with their main carers are best placed to thrive. So why am I tasked with supporting fellow parents on a weekly, sometimes daily basis to remember that they are perfectly capable of meeting their child's developing needs, given that this is indeed the most natural order of things? Because we've been schooled out of believing it.

Wasn't this supposed to be about self-directed learning? Yes, and that's exactly why I've explained the above, because for me, self-directed learning and especially unschooling, is a natural extension of this exact kind of parental input, only it continues past five years old when a child becomes compulsory education age. Sorry, that's four as that's when you are told to enrol your child in school nowadays. Hang on, actually I think it's three as that's when you are now encouraged to send your child to preschool to prepare them for school. Surely it can't be two. Oh wait, you are now told there is free childcare, and you should be using it. At some point I'm guessing you'll be expected to have your child enrolled into some kind of newborn programme as soon as they escape the womb, into the arms of, that's right, your friendly neighbourhood government official. I know that sounds dramatic, but that is genuinely what it feels like at times. This is why I find it so interesting that unschooling in particular is seen as the bad apple or a radical thing threatening to tear down society. It's seen as wild, permissive and everything that is the opposite of what a school system upbringing looks like. Allowing your child to direct their own learning? Whatever next!

It can be easy to assume unschooling and self-directed education is at least permissive, simply because permissive styles of parenting often include actions you might see mentioned around them. However, it has very little in common with the definition of neglectful parenting as this type of parenting is often uninvolved, cold, indifferent, and severely lacking in parental input of any kind. Right now, you might be reading this and thinking 'But unschooling is neglectful?' For those that are having those thoughts I just ask that you remember how ingrained the schooled way of thinking is. I can understand why you might see information about unschooling and immediately jump to it being neglectful because it is just so very disconnected from what we recognise as education. I get it. But I can't lie, I find it ironic given that many families are home educating because state education has become so disconnected from the human beings we are and what we need!

There are of course several sides to everything and while the vast majority of unschooling families are doing an outstanding job, there will also be families who are not and are instead neglecting their children. I personally wouldn't even define those people as home educators, let alone unschoolers but regardless of my thoughts, neglectful and harmful parents do exist in all areas of life, the home education community included and I'm thankful our authorities have appropriate checks and measures in order to intervene if required. Regardless of our own preconceived ideas, there are clear thresholds around what constitutes neglect and educational neglect is a part of that too. Just as there are some excellent teachers, there are also teachers that are in prison unable to be around children for the rest of their lives. Just as there are wonderful parents, there are also those who are cruel and depraved. Just as there are genuine and kind people in the world, we know that the opposite of that is also true. What I do know is that the majority of those who practise unschooling who I've come into contact with, do not seem to neglect their children because neglect would be against the entire basis of their beliefs around what unschooling is. But it does look very different to traditional forms of education and parenting, so I do appreciate concerns.

*Parenting*

Neglectful or uninvolved parenting (as coined by clinical and developmental psychologist Diana Baumrind) has traits aligned with cold and aloof parents who don't do rules, don't engage with their children, don't supervise their children and at times do not meet even basic needs such as shelter, food, or care. It's important to recognise that uninvolved parenting is often unintentional. Parents may be experiencing difficulties that mean they aren't able to give more of themselves to their children or may have experienced this parenting style themselves or not have the skills needed to parent differently. Uninvolved parenting features a low-demand approach, similar to that of unschooling, but far from this being in collaboration with the child, it is low demand due to the unavailability of the parent who may almost be like a stranger to the child.

I also mentioned permissive parenting so let's look at some characteristics, as it has more in common with unschooling. In Permissive parenting, parents are warm and caring, big on autonomy, low demand, super engaged with their children and highly supportive of their needs. These are all similar characteristics of unschooling, so I can completely see why from an outside view unschooling can be mistaken for this parental style. The issue though, comes down to why the parents display these traits.

Unschooling and self-directed learning are very intentional pathways, but I don't believe permissive parenting is. Permissive parents just want their children to be free to enjoy childhood while being shielded from the controls of life and they don't want to be the bad guy by having to be the one in control and taking charge. Understandable right? Parenting is hard. With permissive parenting, there is often a motivation of fear and avoidance leading to low boundaries and inconsistent parental behaviour. Permissive parents often indulge as many of the needs and wants of their children as possible and so when they do need to get their child to engage in something, they might use gifts and treats to soften the blow to their child's autonomy. The issue again is the motivation behind why permissive parents do this. I genuinely don't believe any parent who has ended up in this difficult space of unassertive parenting, chooses to be there. But when we consistently do things to make life easier for us in the moment, it can all build up into a space of becoming fearful of our child's reactions if we were to stop. It is super tricky territory for sure, but also not what I would consider a common issue in unschooling as unschoolers aren't necessarily trying to be their child's peer-level friend and gain their approval, unschooler parenting isn't via fear, it's via connection. There are two other parenting styles that were coined by Diana Baumrind which are Authoritarian and authoritative. Coupled with the others, they feel a little like:

*Uninvolved parenting "Do what you like, I don't care".*

*Permissive parenting "What do you think? How can I help make that happen? Just please don't shout at me".*

*Authoritarian parenting "Do as I say or suffer the consequences".*

*Authoritative parenting "Let's find a way that feels more respectful to your thoughts while still making you do what I need you to do".*

I don't know about you, but I actually find authoritative parenting to be the most dishonest one, as despite how horrendous other styles can be, at least you know where you stand with them. With authoritative parenting, there is often an undertone of sneakiness that I just can't get on board with. It's the way in which children are more respected and encouraged to give their own thoughts and opinions but ultimately the parents' rules stand regardless. It reminds me a little of work reviews. You know, where the manager empathises with your struggles while knowing that they won't be making any changes, even if they could anyway. However, at least with the authoritative approach, children are granted much more understanding, patience, and support than others. As you can imagine, the authoritative style has the highest support for good reason. It strikes a balance between meeting the child's needs and maintaining strong boundaries and expectations. Parents are caring and supportive, highly engaged in their children's lives while also having consistent rules and expectations around how children should behave. This style expects children to have opinions on the things that affect them and respects that they may not agree with the parents' decisions.

So, you are probably now expecting me to sell unschooling and self-directed education to you as the holy grail of parenting, right? Well prepare to be disappointed because it has its own issues too. Unschooling is outside of general societal norms and can therefore lead to parents and children feeling disconnected or isolated, due to others not being able to connect to something so far outside of conventional comfort zones. Home education itself is poorly understood, let alone an approach that encompasses whole family life and does away with almost everything we are schooled to believe we must do!

Unschooling in particular can also be heavily dogmatic with principles presented as absolute fact that must be followed for you to be able to class yourself as an unschooler and is ironically sometimes reminiscent of school mum cliques or school-based cliques. On top of that, unschooled children can also sometimes feel like the odd one out amongst peers who are parented and educated in more traditional ways. It's not exactly the picnic you envision, is it. But what I love about the concept is how it's based in an ethos of mutual respect, autonomy, and trust. Unschoolers are warm, caring, and supportive of their children. They are respectful of their child's autonomy and highly engaged in their children's lives, aiming to provide the right environment in which their child can flourish in their own way, rather than in a way parents expect and want. Unschoolers do this by being present, open, and curious about their child so that they can accommodate and partner the child on their journey through childhood into adulthood. They often do a lot of personal development, unpicking their own experiences and conditioning so that they are better able to be available to their children without pushing as many of their own mindsets and expectations onto them. Unschooled children and parents have their views and opinions heard and respected as the autonomous humans they are and because of this, families typically have less arbitrary rules, but with a focus on each person respecting the boundaries of others in the home. Rather than parents imposing punishments, consequences come naturally in connection with the actions of each person and support and understanding is given when difficulties arise. Parents adopt a role of coach and mentor encouraging their children to explore the world and make meaning from it in their own ways with parents on hand to facilitate that exploration so that the children can get everything they need from it. It's the style that most aligns with how we do things in our house; an ever-changing balancing act between unpicking my own reactions, maintaining my own boundaries, being present and curious in my children's lives and facilitating it all so that everyone can thrive. Far from being neglectful or permissive, I've found that this approach requires us as parents to expect more of ourselves so that we can show up in the best ways for ourselves and our children. By approaching parenting from a space of being a guide and coach to our children, you accept that they are their own people who need your support and modelling, to partner them as they grow and develop. But to do this you must come from a place of trust which is no easy feat, I can tell you! Trusting that humans are hardwired to learn and grow from birth onwards isn't easy when you've been schooled to believe that from 5 years old, they need something more than freedom to explore and partnership. Interestingly, with young children we encourage all of the things unschoolers do naturally. But once children grow past a certain age? Play and freedom to explore are replaced with a top-down approach of what we adults have decided children need instead. For me, unschooling merely questions why and explores what might happen if we threw away that particular rule book. In conclusion, I'd say unschooling is the opposite of neglectful parenting. But it's also not authoritarian either.

It is low demand, yet connective. It's engaged yet not overly helicopter parenting. It's somewhere deep in the spaces, in-between all the rules others decided and instead it paves a way for supporting children into adulthood with autonomy, respect, and trust in them to learn as the amazing human beings they are.

## *Time for a breather!*

Well done! Listening to me wax lyrical about a special interest of mine is never an easy task, so congrats for getting through it. How will you celebrate?

For this chapter's reflection, I simply want you to consider where you are on your home education journey right now. Is it working for everyone? Is it providing what you wanted home ed to provide?

How do you feel about self-directed learning right now? Has it changed since reading the last chapter? It's okay if it hasn't and it's important to know that just because autonomous self-directed learning works best for my family, it doesn't mean it works well for every family. That's the beauty of our community, we each do our best for our families however that looks as we change and grow.

**P.s. grab a snack as the next chapter is a beast.**

# Neurodivergence, educational needs and home education

When I first began home educating, I had no idea how much I would learn about my own children, their neurodivergence, their educational needs and myself. I also didn't expect to learn as much as I have about the world of neurodivergence, educational needs and disability as a whole. This chapter is a beast. Some of it is ranty, and some of it is wordy, so I'd advise you to take it a little at a time, especially if you have a neurodiverse family. It's a lot.

Firstly, a note about the term SEN or special education needs. It's a legal term and so while you will see it used in context here, please know that I find the use of the term really poor, along with the idea of additional needs. Individual need's yes but additional or special ones, it's a no from me! Every child has individual needs, every single one and it's only because of the ablest society we live in, that some of those needs are classified as 'special' or 'additional'. Some of a child's needs are general and related to age, such as a small child needing a pushchair or stool as they cannot walk as far or reach as high. We see these are expected needs. Others are individual to the child such as their own preferences, likes or dislikes and others relate to a child's individual way of exploring the world, accessing the world, or understanding it such as needing support, reassurance, tools, or resources. Again, as a society we see most of these as the normal, expected needs of developing children. We provide the accommodations needed because we can see there are everyday life barriers preventing the child from accessing the thing. We do this because children are expected to need support. I want to be clear that I'm not saying this to minimise the challenges of those with educational needs or disabilities, their needs are very real, individual, and important. It's just they aren't special or additional, they are simply the needs of that individual child. All children have a right to have their individual needs met. Sadly, my view is one that often causes society to glitch out with cries of *"But how else will we identify those in need of support? We need to single them out as special, so we can include them..."*. I would argue that considering it is our society that creates the biggest barriers of access for disabled people, that instead we could ya know, just make society more equitable and then less barriers would exist for everyone. But hey ho, we live and dream.

You see when it comes to a child's individual needs in mainstream education, things often then become seen from a medical model of disability. The world of education classifies a child as having special education needs or a disability if the child has a significantly greater difficulty in learning than the majority of others of the same age or has a disability which prevents or hinders them from making use of facilities for others of the same age, in mainstream school. What this model does is to put the focus on the child being the odd one out. It's the child who has significant difficulty learning or the child who cannot access the facilities. It's not the way the learning or facilities have been set up that are at fault, but the child trying to access them. It tells us that education happens in a particular way and those who cannot access it are broken. The person is seen as the issue rather than the way society is run and organised.

School buildings, the school system and the school curriculum were designed by neurotypical, non-disabled people for neurotypical, non-disabled children and I understand why. The school system itself was set up in an era where those who were disabled were presumed to be unable to learn and as sad as that is, that was simply the understanding we had at the time but as the great Maya Angelou famously stated "Do the best you can until you know better. Then, when you know better, do better." We have come a long way since the days of placing disabled children in institutions, but my word do, we still have a long way to go. What I struggle with most is that in 2023, we really do know better yet we are facing one of the worst crises in failing disabled children with thousands of children unable to access suitable education.

Over time, society has developed better tools to enable us to distinguish when a child is having challenges and we are now at a place where the number of children recognised as having educational needs or disabilities is super high. This is not an epidemic nor a trend. This is simply the result of better tools and a better societal understanding of the development of children. Back when society thought disabled people existed in very small numbers and that they weren't able to learn, I could understand them not being accommodating. *In 2023 the number of children registered in schools as being SEN stood at approximately 1.5 million. With approximately 9 million children in school, this leaves us with a current education system that is unsuitable for approximately 17% of all students.*[4]

In real terms this equates to around 4 - 5 students in every class. Disabled children exist in every classroom. Children with educational needs exist in every classroom. They are high in number and yet low in getting their educational needs met. These children are not the problem, the school system is. Here is a simple example. My daughter has attended school for 5 years. The building is an old building with tall slim corridors and doorways. The classrooms are typically high ceilings but small in terms of floor space and the building is set out over 2 floors with various outbuildings. There is no lift to gain access to the second floor. The entrance to reception is a single width door. The corridor doorways are double width, but the classroom doorways are typically slim as with Victorian style buildings. Because of the high ceilings, all sound (even the smallest whisper) reverberates as if in a concert hall. Classrooms are packed with information on every wall, tables are packed closely together, and, in most classrooms, they feature a wall of tall multi pane windows that cause light to dance around the room. Just the building itself is all out inaccessible for wheelchair users and is a nightmare for deaf students, autistic and adhd students and visually impaired students. I know that it's possible to design and renovate school buildings to work differently because my husband

---

[4] SEN students 2023 https://explore-education-statistics.service.gov.uk/find-statistics/special-educational-needs-in-england

often attends other schools on maintenance visits across the country and notes the things these schools do well. But instead, the government pushes a painfully routine rhetoric that the majority of mainstream schools are actually entirely suitable for all children thanks to the SEND system.

This SEND system makes schools and local authorities responsible for providing accommodations to help disabled children access the mainstream curriculum / system / building and this is possibly the farthest we've ever come as a society towards recognising disabled people as persons equal of a good education,  but rather than provide an education system that is actually suitable to all children, with curriculums and systems and buildings that make sense to disabled children's needs and thus to everyone's needs, we aim to place sticking plasters over the worst bits and single out disabled students as needed something extra. That something extra comes via classroom accommodations, school accommodations, SEN units attached to mainstream schools or special schools. The issue with this is that classroom and school accommodations don't work for the vast majority of children with educational needs and or disabilities, SEN units are harder to access than a child needing a wee mid lesson and special school places are Goldust and are only actually suitable for specific students. For example, my children never needed a special school, they simply needed a school able to accommodate them in real terms, rather than with niceties and false promises.

*Confession time*

I have one child who has a rare medical condition. As a rule, the school system has standards and expectations on attendance that he was unable to meet due to regular hospital visits, weeklong investigations at Great Ormond Street, higher than average sick days etc. The school itself accommodated his needs by understanding this was just a part of this individual child's needs. The system, on the other hand, sent me letters telling me how much education my child was missing and how I must do better. Ironically these letters would come while he was spending many of his days in the finest educational museums in London. The school accommodated us by telling me to ignore the letters while also saying they weren't able to stop sending them out and then making my medically unwell son sit in 100% attendance certificate assemblies knowing he would never receive one himself.

My eldest child had access to the school's SEN unit, where she thrived with her individual learning pod, access to fidget toys and play based learning. Right up until they decided she was doing so well; they couldn't justify her having access anymore and she needed to be integrated back into the mainstream classroom. (This was pre EHCP) Her reward for being accommodated and able to access education in a way suitable for her, was to then take it away as if this accommodation had fixed her lifelong autistic brain.

My second eldest was given accommodations in secondary school such as a toilet pass, a pass to leave the classroom to go to the SEN unit, a pass to leave early for lunch. She was allowed the accommodation of wearing her headphones at all times. Only, when she then used those passes, she was sometimes questioned, refused, argued with. The entire point of the pass was to be able to show it to the teacher and then leave without comment, with the teacher then knowing where she was heading. She was regularly refused early leave for lunch, despite it being specifically in her SEN plan, meaning she then simply didn't eat as it was too busy, loud, and overwhelming. She was regularly told to remove her headphones and threatened with confiscation, despite them being on her SEN plan and then the school wondered why she ended up spending the majority of her final year going straight to the SEN unit daily instead. Rant over, let's get back to it.

These are just some of the reasons we home educate and why home education is sometimes the best option and at other times, the only option to enable a parent to meet their legal duty, because leaving your child in a school that is not providing them with a suitable education for them, is a failure on us to meet our duty. I know that sounds extreme but it's the simple truth. Whether our children are in school or home educated, our duty is to ensure they receive a suitable education. When we can see our child is not being provided with what they need, we have a duty to act. We can act by working with the school, working with the SEN and EHCP system, fighting for our child's right to access an education within the school system, or by focusing on providing the education in a way other than via school. I've tried all of the above over many years and I've come to understand that my duty is to my child. The battles I pick, must have them as my central focus and so home education was eventually the only choice as well as being the first choice for the youngest. That certainly doesn't mean that home ed is perfect, but it was better than leaving my children in a school that could not accommodate even their most basic needs.

*What is SEND?*

I've spoken a tonne about SEN, educational needs and disability above so let's look at the definitions. SEND is the acronym of Special Educational Needs and Disabilities.

Some children and adults have learning difficulties and / or disabilities. Learning difficulties are super common. Disabilities are common. Learning disabilities are less so. A child can also be disabled and experience learning difficulties but not have any learning disabilities. Long term conditions such as epilepsy, asthma, diabetes, and cancer also fall under disabilities. Being disabled does not necessarily mean a child will also have a special educational need, but disabilities can often overlap with learning difficulties and learning disabilities, so if your child is disabled, they will usually fall under SEN provision.

Note - This part of the chapter does contain medical terms and medical model views of disabilities. The reason for this is that these are the terms you will most likely hear in relation to your children. It doesn't mean I agree with the terms or definitions, just that it's helpful to know the legal and medical terms that will often be used.

**Disability**

The Equality Act 2010 defines a disabled person as someone who has a physical or mental impairment that has a 'substantial' and 'long-term' negative effect on their ability to do normal daily activities. It's important to recognise that just because someone has a disability, it doesn't mean that the person will also have an intellectual or learning disability. People with disabilities may have several conditions, disabilities, difficulties, or none.

## Learning disabilities

Learning disabilities relate to how challenging it is for the child or adult to learn, take in and use new information. There are several conditions that make it more likely to have learning and intellectual disabilities alongside the condition. Learning disabilities can be as a result of being born with a condition, genetics, childhood illness, birth trauma such as lack of oxygen, brain injury and many other examples. It's important to understand that having a learning disability doesn't mean the person cannot learn, it instead means it can be difficult and challenging for the person and they may need support in some or all areas of life. Some of the more common conditions that make it more likely for someone to also experience learning or intellectual disabilities are Down's syndrome, Williams syndrome, Autism, Fragile X syndrome, Cerebral palsy, Global development delay.

## Learning difficulties

Learning difficulties relate more to accessing educational content, environments, and institutions. A child or adult with learning difficulties does not necessarily have intellectual disabilities and it's instead that the way in which the world is set up to learn, creates barriers of access for the person. It's possible for someone to have both a learning disability and a learning difficulty or to have one and not the other. Common learning difficulties are dyslexia, dyscalculia, developmental coordination disorder (dyspraxia), sensory integration disorders, auditory processing disorders, language processing disorders, neurodevelopmental disorders, executive function disorders. A physically disabled child may also be classed as having a learning difficulty if they are unable to access the school environment due to the environment not being disability friendly.

**Disability, further definitions**

In general terms disability tends to fall under four main areas; intellectual, physical, sensory, mental but this sits differently in relation to children and the SEND code of practice. There are also many other types of disability not falling under these main umbrella terms too, so it's helpful to understand the four main areas of disability and the four broad SEND areas of need. We will also explore an additional area of disability, neurodevelopmental disabilities. Disability definitions tend to focus on the diagnosis or medical area of disability whereas SEND tends to focus on the educational needs of the child, regardless of any diagnosis. First let's look closer at disability definitions.

**Intellectual disabilities** are disabilities relating to the way in which a person's brain learns, functions, and retains information. Some people are born with intellectual disabilities and others acquire them in a number of ways such as brain injury as one example.

**Physical disabilities** relate to a person's mobility, dexterity, stamina, and ability to use their body to perform tasks. These can be temporary or permanent.

**Sensory disabilities** relate to the way in which a person processes information with their senses. Most commonly these disabilities relate to the function of a person's eyes and ears such as visual or hearing impairment but can involve disabilities in any of the senses such as sensory processing disorders.

**Mental disabilities** relate to a person's mental health. These types of disabilities are often psychiatric conditions such as schizophrenia, bipolar affective disorder, anxiety disorders, depression, obsessive compulsive disorder, dementia, eating disorders. Emotion based school avoidance (EBSA) encompasses several aspects of mental health disability.

**Additionally Neurodevelopmental disabilities**. These relate to what is classed as disorders of the nervous system, including the brain. These are called neuro developmental because they relate to the nervous system and how it develops in ways different to what would be expected as a child grows. In medical terms they are disorders of brain function that affect emotion, learning ability, self-control and memory which unfolds as an individual develops and grows. Some common neurodevelopmental disabilities and difficulties are Autism, ADHD, communication, speech and language disorders, intellectual disabilities, motor disorders such as tic disorders and developmental coordination disorder (dyspraxia), dyslexia, dyscalculia. Traumatic brain injury, fetal alcohol syndrome disorders. Neurogenetic disorders are also under the umbrella of neurodevelopmental disorders. Children with neurodevelopmental disabilities grow into adults with neurodevelopmental disabilities, these are not something a person grows out of. Children may have intellectual, sensory, physical, and mental disabilities alongside their neurodevelopmental disorders, or none but many will have needs across all 4 of the broad-spectrum areas of SEND needs.

## SEND code of practice 2014

Let's look at the SEND code of practice 2014. This sets out the 4 broad areas of need relating to SEND. These are:

### Communication and interaction needs.

These are speech, language, and communication needs.

### Cognition and learning needs.

These are learning needs ranging from moderate learning difficulties (MLD) through to profound and multiple learning difficulties. (PMLD) as well as Specific learning difficulties (SpLD)

### Emotional, social, mental health needs

These are needs that relate to social wellbeing, behaviour and emotional health with mental health conditions featuring as well as social and emotional needs.

### Sensory and / or physical needs

These are needs that are sensory such as visual and or hearing impairment, sensory processing disorders or physical disabilities that relate to mobility, stamina, use of one's body.

Some children may have a single specific learning difficulty which entitles them to SEN provision and others may have conditions that mean they fall under both learning difficulties and disabilities, spanning all 4 broad areas of the SEND code of practice, but every child whether they have SEND or not, is entitled to access a suitable education by law.

*Why does any of this matter regarding your home-ed child?*

As parents we have a duty to ensure that our children receive an efficient, full-time education suitable to their age, aptitude, ability, and any special educational needs they may have. This is applicable whether your child is in a school or home educated. When we are home educating a child who has been to school and has educational needs or disabilities these children often also have experienced trauma and may be burnt out and needing to avoid demands. Because of this the approach often needs to look very different to a school education and while that is the beauty of home education, it can also be scary and overwhelming for us as parents. Typically, as new home edders we will first try to drop into types of home ed that more closely align to school based practices simply because that's what we know. But because these specific children are already in deeply distressed states, that's just not going to work. Instead, we often need to approach education in a trauma informed way. First, we need to work to establish safety so that the child is able to regulate out of a heightened state, only then offering choice and collaboration while we model that we can be trusted to support them in ways that they need, before being able to begin empowering them in their learning journey.

## Confession time

When I deregistered one of my children they had only been in school until they were 6. Despite this, they had a huge amount of distrust in me. Every time I allowed a teacher to drag him off my legs, I betrayed him. Every time I invested in the school's approach to getting him into school, I betrayed him. I was his one safe space and that had been broken. Now, it's important to say that I was doing what I thought was right at the time and was following the advice of the experts. I don't blame myself for this, but whether intentions were pure or not, my child had been traumatised and it took a lot of work to heal that. It took years. Years of me doing what I say and saying what I do. Years of being specific and sticking to that. Years of promises not being broken or pushed further. It took 3 years for him to actually attend a specific home ed event fully and we took it each week at a time. First, we talked about going. Then we went and sat in the car quite far away. Then we parked closer. Then we sat outside the car. Then we sat nearby etc. At every single step he was in charge of how far we went, how long we stayed, and I responded each time to his needs. That child now trusts me again. He trusts me to advocate for him, to listen to him and to work with him and he will generally give most things a go, more than once, knowing I've got his back. But my word it took time, compassion, and patience. Confession over, let's get back to it.

This is all well and good but in the back of your mind, you know you need to be providing a full time suitable education and because of this, it can be really overwhelming and worrying when you consider how you would show that the child is currently receiving a suitable education in those early weeks and months or even years, if and when the LA make informal inquiries. That's why it's really important that you are aware and confident in the law and guidelines around home education, but also SEND. Remember, suitable education is not only suitable to the child's age, but also to their ability and SEN. A traumatised child may be 13 in age and in an un traumatised state have similar abilities to other 13-year-olds, but their special educational needs set them apart from the norm. What instead becomes important is how that the child is making progress in line for them and their needs. In children with complex needs your aims for their education is an important part of home ed. It sets out what you believe education is for, but more specifically what you hope to achieve regarding this specific child's education and that will be different for every child because education should be different for every child.

A child who has educational needs and or disabilities should have an education that focuses on:

- Their needs and how these needs can be best met rather than school-based views of education.

- Recognising that education takes place in lots of different ways and that informal learning will be happening, even in a distressed state.

- Recognising that the learning might be conversational or informally observed and that this is just as valid as any other form of learning.

- Recognising that emotional wellbeing is a precursor to the ability to take in and retain new information and so your child may be needing familiar and less challenging learning while finding safety.

- Recognising that consolidation of learning is an important part of education.

- Recognising that educational aims that do not follow a school-based age-related focus are not wrong or a failure to provide an education.

And it should focus on providing an education that is tailored to the child themselves and how they can be supported to grow into an independent member of society, however that will look for them.

Home education for a child with complex needs can be challenging. But it's not because the child is unable, or because education isn't happening. It's because until we meet them where they are at, they cannot get any further. We as parents must learn about our child from them, rather than those who purport to be the experts of them. We must see our children as the experts on themselves and find ways that help them feel safe and able and capable. And most importantly we must learn to recognise the education that's actually taking place over a school-based approach that didn't work for them in the first place.

## Time for a breather

Education is complex and even more so when your child has disabilities or challenges accessing that education. Snacks help. I mean, snacks always help no matter what, I find.

Let's take a moment to reflect on the last chapter. Supporting specific educational needs is complex, especially when it comes to state education, but I find that actually, home education often simplifies this. I feel this is because as parents, we naturally provide the kinds of accommodations and support that we can see our children need, to be able to flourish and thrive. This is provided intuitively and via the natural assessing that we consciously and unconsciously do as parents. This might look very different to what would be provided in a school and that's okay. Accommodating your child's needs doesn't mean they won't grow or learn or thrive for more. There is a belief parroted in the educational world that if a child is given 'too much' accommodation, they won't learn to push themselves or become resilient. Contrary to this belief accommodations actually *enable* children to thrive because they have what they need to get where they want to go and are fully supported to do so.

Whether your child has specific educational needs or not take a moment to think about how as a parent you already provide much of what your child needs, naturally.

Think about the moments your child has struggled with something and how you've helped them to get through that.

Think about the moments your child has shown frustration or upset at a task and how you've coached and supported them.

P.s. A note on resilience. Disabled children already experience the toughest of circumstances just in their day to day lives. The world is not made for them and yet, they find a way to participate. They find a way to learn and grow with the right support. If they are really struggling with something, its usually on top of the other 100 things they naturally struggle with daily. They don't need more resilience. These kids could provide a TEDtalk on that subject. No, they need our understanding, our love and most of all, us to advocate for them when the world is too much, so they can keep keeping on in their awesomeness.

Okay. Go eat some cake. Take a walk in the fresh air, feel the wind or rain against your skin. Whatever it is you need to do right now so you can show up as the best parent you strive to be daily, keep doing it. You rock.

# Home Educating Teens

Baking and woodland walks are wonderful and a firm foundation of many home ed lives. But let's be honest, as your children grow there is only so much baking you can do and still call it numeracy once those fundamental skills are well and truly 'baked' in (couldn't resist) So, what does home ed look like for older children? Does it need to become more formal? Is it possible to still do very little 'book work'? Let's dig in. That's right, it's time to discuss the terrifying prospect of home educating children who no longer shriek with joy at a tub of sand and water; the ever elusive and frequently misunderstood enigma that is a teenager.

In some respects, home ed is easy when your children are under 12. They are learning new things daily, there are huge spurts of development and growth, and their brains are sponges soaking up new experiences to make meaning of. Every day feels like a fresh adventure and there is so much learning happening, just by your children being the inquisitive, awe-inspiring humans they are, that it could almost be a challenge to fit in a more formal approach even if you wanted to! They are learning about the world for the first time and everything that goes with it. By the time these children reach around 12 they've got some really solid grounding in what the world is made up of, who they are, how things work and some generally fab foundations. This is usually when as parents we begin to worry, because we feel like we are running out of stuff to teach them.

You see, when it comes to the act of actually home educating, a huge proportion of the information available tends to gear itself towards younger children. You may have gone looking for resources and found lots of hands on, play based learning for children under eleven but discovered a distinct lack of that same stuff tailored to children over eleven. That in itself needs a healthy dose of deschooling. The idea that once a child reaches a certain age, they then need to invest their time in a structured and prescribed form of academic study is a hangover from school-based mindsets and needs to get in the bin.

When your baby was born, you were the one engaging them in play, helping them to grow and learn about their little world. When they were toddlers, you were the one encouraging them to communicate and walk and jump in puddles and play. When they were a little older, you were the one answering every question and encouraging more with all the stuff you were introducing into their world, while they played and had fun. Then came the pre-teens. You were the one chatting to them about books they've read and toys they love and taking them to their clubs and groups or getting the resources they needed to do the things they love to have fun with learning and keep playing. Now you have teens and none of that needs to change. You can still be the one partnering their adventures, sharing the world with them, helping them to grow and learn and have fun. You can still be the one exploring and playing and failing and trying and having a laugh with them, while they do it. You do not need to change to formal education just because you now have a teen. You don't suddenly need to outsource to tutors or curriculums or online schools. Because all humans learn so much more when they are enjoying what they are doing and having fun with it, no matter their age. Home educating a teenage child is almost exactly the same as home edding a younger child. It's only what we've been taught about education that holds us back from recognising it. Teens still have a drive to play, explore, learn, and grow in exactly the same ways as younger children, they just use very different resources and approaches to do it.

Your experience of home educating a teen will massively depend on how long you've been home educating that specific child, whether they've experienced trauma or difficulties in school, whether they've always been home ed, whether they have any specific needs and so much more. There is no one size fits all and as your home edder gets older, panic can set in and push us parents out of our comfort zones, causing us to worry that they won't be successful or amount to anything because they are getting closer to 16 and haven't followed a similar path to others.

This idea of success in relation to education is one of the things that saddens me. Children are shoved on the conveyor belt of the school system with excitement and joy and an overwhelming majority come out 12 years later, stressed and tired with zero desire to continue with anything educational, yet the government's cure for this drop in engagement was not to look at the research and evidence of their failings, no, their solution was to raise the participation age to 18 and try to force 16 year olds into further education, employment and/or training for another 2 years.

Friends, the education system in the UK isn't even getting the basics right. Our young people are spending longer and longer in education, yet attainment of basic skills is falling. The OECD skills review in 2016[5] showed that in 2013 an estimated 9 million UK adults had low numeracy and/ or literacy skills and worse than that it showed that the skills of younger people (16-19) are reducing. In most countries literacy and numeracy skills in young people are stronger than those heading towards retirement. In the UK this is not the case and is actually the opposite. Those nearing retirement in the UK have stronger basic skills than those in younger age brackets. This means that in time, the basic skills of our labour force will continue to degrade causing significant issues for our economy in the future. The OECD recommends that UK schools must improve basic education provided to children of school age if they want to address the issue and that although the more recent reforms of raising the participation age and adding a requirement of numeracy and literacy study alongside further education is good, these do not have the same benefits and impacts as getting the foundations right in the first place.

Given that home educators account for less than 1 percent of school age children, I'm going to guess that we probably aren't the problem when it comes to failures around adults in the UK having poor literacy and numeracy skills and even if every home ed child was functionally illiterate, that would still only account for around 1.5%, leaving the other 98.5%

---

[5] OECD Building skills for all: A review of England
https://unesdoc.unesco.org/ark:/48223/pf0000245675

coming from school education. Somehow a few still manage to suggest it's a reason to have more oversight on home education anyway though of course, and yes, I'm looking at you, Education Select Committee 2021.[6] Why am I telling you all of this and what has it got anything to do with home educating teens, well I guess it's to make a point.

Who is more likely to succeed in attaining the basic skills of numeracy and literacy...

- A teen who is one of 12 million in the school system of a country who are failing to increase the basic skills of our younger population.

- A teen who has a 1 in 3 chance of passing English and maths at GCSE level simply because that's how the system works?

- A home ed teen who has the support and one to one attention and encouragement of their parents, regardless of said parents own basic skills?

Answers on a postcard because that's right, we have a winner! It's the home ed teen. More specifically, your home ed teen. As you might remember from a previous chapter, school teens in the UK are more anxious, depressed and stressed than ever before. That is not a conducive environment for learning and not an environment we would want to replicate at home, so how do we marry up the need to ensure our young people have skills required for

---

[6] Strengthening Home Education Report 2021
https://publications.parliament.uk/pa/cm5802/cmselect/cmeduc/8
4/8402.htm

independent life, while not contributing to the pandemic of mental health issues in existence today? Honestly, I'm no genius but I really do think it's pretty simple and I have a living example in my own now grown young person, as well as knowing that her experience is not outside of the norm for home-ed teens.

My eldest child became home-ed when she was 11 years old. She always struggled with school but secondary was where we just got to the point of deciding that was enough and so she was deregistered towards the end of the second term. We began with a period of deschooling with her wanting to play a lot of computer games and do not much else. I was new to home education and still had these hilarious ideas of deschooling being a few months and that would be it. 6 months in I began to panic but we kept going. She was engaged, learning, and interested in stuff for the first time in ages so I kept on unpicking my own mindsets around gaming not being educational. By around 8 months in she was voluntarily taking herself to the library weekly and reading through books like water, before then telling me all the amazing things she had learnt. She also agreed to come along to a home ed meet or two regularly and made some friends. After a year she started to play with creating games and graphics herself and found Blender, 3D modelling software, coding and graphic design kept her busy. She designed logos for my business and provided graphics for others too but began to feel like there was more she could be doing and so decided she wanted to upgrade her PC and do some online courses in programming. She designed her PC to meet her specs and created spreadsheets with item comparisons, pricing and a running calculation of money being saved.

About 3 years into home education, she asked to attend a local college who were offering a games design course 1 day a week and off she went! At 15 after completing her level one she decided to apply full time to college as a key stage 4 student. She was nervous as needed to do some assessments in literacy and numeracy and hadn't done any formal learning since she left school, but aced them all, scoring higher than average compared to her peers. She saved for her PC, bought all the parts, put it together and began her level two course full time as an EHE student. By the time she was 18 she had worked her way through games design levels 1, 2 and 3 plus gained a GCSE pass in both English and maths and headed off to Uni so she could keep learning about the subject she loved.

At 20 she is a fully fledged adulting human who now lives independently away from home. She works part time, manages her own finances, manages her time and relationships and is frankly doing an utterly sterling job with all that life has thrown at her. She's left uni for now, knowing that the balance of what is required of her vs. what she can give, is not right for her currently and has placed value on staying healthy, well and enjoying what life can bring instead. She loves her job and the challenges it brings, and she approaches every hiccup in life with thoughtfulness, critical thinking, compassion for herself and a wicked sense of humour. That to me is success. That is the measure of a successful person and a successful education, and do you know what I did differently? I encouraged her to lead the way, however that looked and then made sure she had the tools to build the path she could see ahead, for herself. I also tried hard to stop getting in the way, with my ideas of what I thought that path should look like too.

This is what I think all teens need. I have 3 of them and it's working so far. For me, teens need less instruction and more opportunity for collaboration and to find their mediums of exploration. They need time and space to have fun in their own ways and enjoy themselves. They need people who will cheerlead their ideas and debate their thoughts with interest and non-judgement. They need interested, open and curious parents who are determined to support them in where they want to go, who respect them for the people they are and may become, without putting their own designs on that. Our teens have lived in a world designed for them since before they were born and so they need to have the opportunity to learn the things relevant to the world they will move into as adults.

Home educating teens can and often does involve certifications and qualifications such as GCSEs, A levels or vocational diplomas but that doesn't mean you need to suddenly approach it like school. I know many successful home-ed young people who have studied the 2-year programme for a GCSE in a conversational style, with practice papers being discussed and explored rather than written and only moving to paperwork before the actual exams themselves. I know others who have studied the 2-year GCSE curriculum in less than a year and achieved high grades. I know others who have done many GCSEs for interest over several years and others who have studied the content but never taken the exam. The difference in every single one has been the young person's desire to do the exam with a specific reason in mind whether that's because they are aware those exams are needed for where they want to go, or because they enjoy the subject and want to learn more.

The idea of taking just exams in the things you want or need, is in itself revolutionary when you think about it because the whole 8-10 GCSEs thing in school, where teens are constantly bombarded with GCSE rhetoric, doesn't need to be a thing in home ed. It can if your child wants, but it doesn't need to be. The reason children take so many GCSEs in school is because school must provide a broad and balanced curriculum and GCSEs are proof that this has taken place. It also provides a wide range of potentials for 16-year-olds who have no clue what they want to do. In home education you are under no obligation to provide a broad and balanced education, but you can and there is no obligation to take any GCSEs, but you can. It's beneficial to do at least some form of certification like GCSE in English and maths, or numeracy and literacy such as functional skills if your child is able. Or English, maths, and a few other GCSEs if they are wanting to go onto A levels but if they aren't able, there are plenty of other opportunities and pathways forward for them. Basically, home education is not school and that is the same whether home edding a younger child or a teen.

Home edding a teen looks different for everyone. One thing to take into consideration is whether they went to school or have always been home-ed. Those children who have always been home educated tend to have a very different outlook on their education and life. If they were in school, how long were they there and were there challenges around school that caused you to become home educators? Is there currently mental health struggles or neurodivergence to be considered? These are all questions that will influence what your home education looks like for your teen. For more academically focused teens who are frustrated with school not providing them with what they need study wise, leaving school to become home educated can sometimes be the solution they need to be able to concentrate on their studies. These teens may benefit from a specific space to study, or a curriculum to follow but they will often arrange that themselves by directing their own education. However, although this may be the picture-perfect vision people have in their head for home educating young people, it is rarer than you expect.

Because of the growing issues with the school system, we instead have a large percentage of secondary age children becoming home-ed because of neurodivergent needs not being met or emotionally based school avoidance (EBSA) and no longer having any options left. These children are often highly capable yet unable to attend school regularly due to their needs not being met due to emotional and mental health struggles. Many families experiencing these struggles try for years to support their children to attend school and often the children themselves are desperate to be able to attend too. Families work tirelessly to help their children while dealing with horrendous policies in England around attendance, with threats of fines, court, and children's services intervention. Sadly, these behaviours from our government have only gotten worse, to the point where we are now criminalising parents of children who are clearly needing support and when and if families then deregister, there is often a huge amount of healing to be done. Home ed often looks very different for these teens. They may be experiencing burnout and trauma and needing time and space to feel safe again. With home education they can take their time. You can home ed for as long as is needed for your child, post 16 home ed remains a valid form of full-time education too.

The beauty with home education is that it is tailored and individualised to the child you have in front of you at that moment. Choosing a different path is not failure and the aim of lifelong learning is one that must be considered as most important, rather than arbitrary rules around age related cohorts or exams. Resources for teens can be anything and everything they want to explore. Hands on projects, tech-based exploration, textbooks and cookery, days out or workshops. Anything and everything. I know one teen who is fully immersed in diving. His parents have provided him with the resources to enable him to follow this passion for years, from scuba diving to training in open sea diving. He's worked his way through several certifications and has been offered a full apprenticeship in this area of interest moving forward. Another teen had an interest in computers and how they work, and his parents provided volunteering opportunities with a local fix it hub. This led to engineering and training to move into his chosen field of racing car engineering. Another teen I know has always had a love of music and has followed this through her grades alongside other studies, to be offered placement at the London Music

Institute. Another teen had several GCSEs under her belt before ending compulsory school age, then A levels and hopes to move into politics.

The best advice I can give relating to home educating teens is to work on your relationship. Work on building your connections together. Learn about what your child is exploring, ask them questions because you want to know more of what they love & provide them with more of that. Find ways to let them invite you into their world, because that is the world, they are building for themselves, and you are there to help them get there. As parents we are constantly helping and guiding and supporting our children to understand more about the world and in doing so, they learn. Teen's experience this in the same way but having already laid down some foundations they will be exploring richer and deeper nuances to assist them towards independence. What they learn will rarely be recognised as a specific 'subject' because these teens are just playing, exploring, asking questions, and building their skills. The reason we parents find it hard to link up that learning with a specific subject is because life isn't broken down into subjects. Science and numeracy and literacy and geography and history and creativity and religion and friendships are all learnt together. Baking is science and numeracy and literacy and creativity all mashed together and a developing teen might move into the economics and business skills, health and hygiene certification, workshops on cake decoration, culinary classes, apprenticeships. A walk in an old part of town is geography and history and literacy all mashed together. A teen might develop this into architecture, art, environmental issues, and local culture. A woodland walk is science and geography and history and numeracy, and literacy all mashed together. For a teen this might develop into foraging, orienteering, herbalism, arboriculture, environmental sciences. The list is endless and anything that was fun for a younger child can be built upon for an older one. Learning is a mish mash of everything learnt and explored, all at once and while the school system breaks life learning down into subjects, you don't need to, because you aren't a school. Instead, you are a parent, supporting and facilitating your child to do what that our younger generation does best, learn!

I do get that this all sounds beautiful and probably a bit farfetched given that we've been taught the reality of living with teens is very different. We are taught that teens are sullen, secretive, oppositional, argumentative, and yes, they can and often are all of those things too. The physiological, neurological, and psychological  developments that teens go through are huge and on top of that their inner and outer worlds are shifting. They are wanting and being expected by parents to become more independent while simultaneously struggling with the shifts back and forth between childhood and adulthood and that shift is rarely linear. As parents we continue to place too much societal value on using specific ages to indicate developmental transitions as well, which doesn't help. I've had 3 children reach teenhood so far, with one left to go and every single one was completely different. Behaviours and shifts happened at different times and ages because they are each individual humans with their own strengths and challenges. Throwing out the metaphorical linear handbook of childhood into adulthood and instead simply responding and accommodating the child in front of me, was one of the best things I ever did. Teens are not adults, they are still children who are going through incredible changes and so while it is entirely appropriate and expected to encourage, support, and enable your teens to continue towards adulthood, they won't get to adulthood for quite some time yet.

If anything, I would say teens need more support, more attention, and more understanding rather than less. I'm reminded of my eldest going through a tough time some years ago. She was passionately explaining the issues she was having and then suddenly lay her head on my lap and burst into tears, grieving that she was no longer a small child and that I couldn't simply fix the thing for her. She didn't want me to fix it. She didn't need me to fix it. She just needed to be heard and held because teenhood is hard and you are pulled in so many directions. That kiddo is now the age I was when I gave birth to her and my word, we have amazing and deep conversations about that. Mostly about how she cannot imagine being responsible for another human being at this age. About how hard it is for me as a parent who needs to navigate their child growing and needing to work things out for themselves and how challenging it is as a teen, who needs their parents more than ever but has been taught they shouldn't. So, while yes, we need to step back in some ways to allow our teens the freedom to develop into who they are becoming, we also need to step closer in other ways to support them as they do that. We need to throw away our preconceived and conditioned ideas of what teenagers should look like and instead simply respond to the child we've got.

Your teens are so very young and navigating that while they feel ready to be independent and out in the world is tough. It's tough for them, it's tough for you and no matter how many children you've partnered through teenhood, it is never the same. Be gentle with you as you journey these uncharted waters. Be honest with your teen about how this is challenging for you both and encourage them to be gentle with themselves through it all. They have an entire life ahead of them to work it all out, and they will.

*Snack Break*

Have a think about some of the conditioning you've picked up over the years about what teens are like. Think back to your own teenhood, what was it like for you? What would have helped you then? What throw away comments have you made over the years about stereotypes of teens? What are some wonderful moments you've shared with your teens? What struggles have you supported them with and what did they need from you in that moment? Being a teen is scary stuff for them, and for us! Be gentle with you are you navigate.

# Home education in practice

Home education is genuinely one of the most beautiful, terrifying, freeing, chaotic journeys I didn't know I would be taking, when I had children 20 years ago. Actually, I'm not sure which I find more surprising; that I'm a home educator or that I have been a parent for 20 years, but life does its thing regardless of our expectations doesn't it. What does home education look like in practice, let's explore.

## Stereotypes

Firstly, there are a lot of stereotypes that people conjure in their heads when they hear that someone is a home educator. There is absolutely nothing wrong with being any of the labels below and also, I need to be clear, I am not the idealised (or horrifying) version of a home educator you probably have in your mind. I'm not an earth mother, in flowing organic cotton dresses with long plaited hair and warm friendly eyes. I didn't breastfeed my children, I am not vegan, and I am pro immunisations. Any other misguided stereotypes people think of when you mention home education that I can throw in here? Ah yes, I am not religious, I believe the world is spherical not flat and we do indeed eat processed food and take medicines when needed.

I have attempted to be more earthy at various points, I've been vegetarian most of my life and did have a stint as a vegan, one of my children cannot have immunisations due to allergies but the others have and I am deeply spiritual but no, not religious. You see, all humans are a beautiful mess of contradictions and when we attempt to place them all in one stereotyped box we miss so much of the beauty.

I know home educators who are earth mothers and I also know parents of schooled children who are too. I also know many who are not. I know vegan home educators and vegan school parents. I know home edders who have breastfed and those who haven't. Same with parents of school children. I know parents of all educational choices who are pro or anti immunisations and that is their choice and right. I know home-ed families who are religious and others who are not. Same with school-based friends. I will say I'm not aware of anyone I know believing the world is flat, but even if they did, we all believe in our own things, right? My point is that a stereotypical home-ed mum doesn't exist, but if they did, I would not be it.

What I am is a very quirky, slightly spicy, real, raw, mum doing the best she can for her children in each moment whatever that looks like. But here's a little secret. Every single home educator I've ever met is doing exactly that too and that same concept applies to every parent of schooled children too. Home edders are just other parents you probably wouldn't even look twice at, if it wasn't for the giant backpack and kids dressed in all weather gear during the middle of the day. We are as full of variety as the school gate parents you might come across in a school playground and therefore you might find some home educators that you have lots in common with and others that you have zero in common with, the same as that works in the rest of life too.

The beauty of home ed is that you get more choice. More choice over what you do and when, who you do that with, where you do those things and what values you place on it all. You aren't bound by the societal rules of school where your children are only able to learn alongside their age group. You aren't bound by subjects or time limits on outdoor and indoor activities, and you most certainly are not bound by having a shallow pool of parent friends to choose from via your child's year 'cohort'.

## Friendships

You will find home edders you like and others you don't. Your children will meet home edders they like and others they don't and even with the ones they like, your children will experience difficulties and challenges, arguments and falling outs and you will be there to partner and support them through it, as will the other parents. Because you are more aware and involved in the educational and social side of things, you will be better placed to model essential skills and provide help through difficult friendship issues. I've had many difficult or awkward conversations with other parents when challenges have cropped up and the difference is immense in how much easier it is to support children's social growth when you are actually active within the realm of it happening, rather than getting 2nd hand info from a school or your children's hours or days after something has happened.

Friendships in home ed is something that needs quite a bit of exploration from us parents. The majority of us parents will have gone through the school system and home educators actually make up less than 1% of school age families, so we are a minority in comparison to the school experience. Many of us will have either a romanticised version of what friendships looked like in school for ourselves, or a trauma informed view. Basically, we don't often have a balanced view of what friendships actually look like in school and while time and age proximity is not the same as genuine friendship, it can lead to genuine friendship. What I mean is that there's a higher possibility that you will find friends in the school environment and the reason for this is time and age proximity. In a school environment, you're in the same classes with the same age people which forces you to need to either get along with each other or avoid each other and because it's a daily thing, you're more likely to need to find ways to work with others or bump into somebody and end up realising you've got similar interests and friendships grow from there. It's essentially an artificial friendship generator and it is the only model in which this kind of socialising is expected and encouraged.

Friendships outside of school look very, very different. When you leave the school environment, you are suddenly chucked into a reality where the proximity friend generator doesn't work. There are people of all ages around you. Age is no longer the deciding factor on who you can be friends with. Adults are not necessarily the authority. You might go on to college with people between 16-19 or even older students in the same classes, you might go on to work with people of all ages, you might go on to a training programme or an apprenticeship. Friendships and building relationships with others suddenly becomes much more complex than it was in school. While the artificial environment of school provides some useful skills such as learning how to negotiate and collaborate with people that you don't necessarily get along great with, it doesn't provide you with a realistic awareness and skill set for being out in the 'real world'.

The reason I'm talking about this is because home education and friendships are extremely different to the artificial proximity friendships that happen in a school environment. In home education, you don't necessarily see the same people every day and they are unlikely to all be the same age even if you did. Year groups and key stages matter far less than you would think and often only relate to specific study groups or tutoring. Home-ed parents also need to be far more proactive in ensuring opportunities are available to their children, because there is no big building full of other children for you to send your child to daily.

With home ed you will be considering whether your child is super social and loves being around others or isn't and enjoys the quiet company of a few chosen friends, or actually prefers their own company. Your child's personality isn't something that is very often considered because with school, you just have to go to school every day, get through it and your own personal preferences aren't really a consideration. Each child is unique and so how they wish to be around others and develop their understanding of society and their place in it, will also be unique. Something else you quickly realise is that your personality will suddenly matter more too! You might be someone who loves to be around other people or someone who gets energy from being on your own or being with small groups of people. If you're not a particularly sociable person, that's completely okay but if you've got a child who is a very sociable person, you will need to find ways to meet that child's needs while also meeting your own. The same applies the other way round too. This is without bringing trauma, disabilities, or neurodivergence into the mix.

As humans we're naturally developed to be around tribes of various different aged people with different skills and expertise. We are best able to learn and grow in those environments, but this has been interfered with via the school system and the way in which we have come to view healthy child development as a hierarchy. Because of this, families can often flounder when new to home ed and finding their feet and finding home educators who they gel with can also be a challenge. It takes more than one meet up. I'm gonna say that much! For example, we've been home educating for nearly 10 years, and I am still getting to know some of the families that we spend time with every week. We spend a few hours a week together at various things and the children have developed some really good friendships over time. With some friends that might be just spending those few hours together, for others it might be that time plus more in other ways. They have friends that are older, friends that are younger, they have interests, passions and joys that mean that they might be friendly with adults who hold interests in those areas where it's not about the age, it's about the interest. Some children are real homebodies and like to see people in their own home every so often or they might prefer to have family as friends. There are other children who struggle being around people face to face, but really enjoy online conversations. I've got a child who's in various different discord servers and has amazing friendships with other teens all over the world. They might never meet those people in person, but it doesn't make their friendship any less important.

## Organisation

How much organisation and planning you require will depend a lot on the style of home ed you are using along with any other commitments you have too but something worth noting is that you will become a PA for your children. You will be taking them to events, ensuring they have copious snacks, drinks, favourite comfort items, giving an itinerary of the event, who will be there, who won't etc. You'll also be finding said events, meetups, and groups to take them to. A lot will also depend on what you have available to give, in time, energy and money. For example, home edding on a low budget is entirely possible but there is still a cost. Generally, if there is a lower financial cost this will often mean a higher time and energy cost. Generally, the higher cost items such as full curriculums, online school etc will need lower time and energy for the parent. Free resources are available on almost everything, but they might require you to put your time and energy into researching, exploring, trying them out,  checking the accuracy, using them as an idea base to create something better aligned to your child etc. Low-cost resources tend to be really good, but some may require you to check accuracy, edit and recreate etc. Medium cost can often be higher accuracy and may have a range of approaches meaning less time and energy needing to individualise it to your child. High-cost resources are sometimes better regulated and are often able to be aligned to your specific requirements (but not always).

In some cases - you might dive into a high-cost item then find it doesn't work for your child and this results in a triple whammy of time, energy, and finances. Simply put, when you are home ed there will always be a cost and that tends to be either financial or time/energy but the cost of home ed is subjective and not really avoidable so it's best to work out what you can afford...whether that's time, energy, money or all three. You will also buy far too many resources and never use them. There will be suitable amounts of panic buying what you will soon come to realise are useless resources that you will never use, despite veteran home edders advising you not to. These items will normally sit gathering dust in a corner of the 'home ed' area you also will never use and worse, you will soon be advising new home edders not to panic buy resources like you did, knowing they are not going to listen. You will be super organised and feeling really accomplished and then approximately 8-10 weeks into home education there will likely be a complete and utter parental meltdown, then again, a few more months in, then a few years. This meltdown will normally include believing you've made the wrong choice, that you're ruining your child's life and that they will never learn anything. These are called the wobbles and are completely natural and normal. Just rinse and repeat while acknowledging that the reality of home education and being truly responsible for your child's education is sometimes fear inducing. Around this same 8–10-week parental meltdown your children may also have reached their peak in terms of behaviours you knew happened but hadn't really experienced full time due to them being in school. Nothing will get done and all your amazing charts and timetables and schedules have been thrown out the window but when you get past this mountain and are gentle with yourselves, things will often begin to improve both for you and your child. Just remember, it's always darkest before dawn, right?

## Resources

As a home ed family having a well-resourced home goes with the territory and there has never been more on offer to home ed families than there is today. But it does mean that you can end up signing up to all sorts and then suddenly realising stuff has been sitting there gathering dust. You might think to yourself 'well that clearly wasn't the right thing for us' and throw it all out. I beg you to please find a random home for all those unused items because they are far more valuable to your child than you think! Take Kiwi kits. We used to get Kiwi kits every month a while back. For about a year a kit came through the post every month and excited hands grabbed the boxes, throwing the contents on the table and getting stuck in immediately. Right up until they didn't. A few months went by when I began to notice I was the one picking the boxes up from the mat, I was the one asking the kids if we were gonna open them. And then it clicked. The kits had finished meeting a need for now. I gathered up the unused kits and put them away, cancelling the subscription as we had amassed several left unopened. Over time the interests the children had, had been met by the kits and so they dropped into other interests. It didn't mean the kits were wrong. In fact, I'd argue they were actually perfect! I kept the unopened kits in the back of a cupboard until while having a tidy, one of the children found those unopened kits and immediately a spark was reignited.

He grabbed all the kits out and put them up on the shelf for easy access. He then pulled one down and (with support) he made a catapult arcade. After building it, he played the game for around 5 minutes, before disappearing off to play Roblox. The making was what he was interested in. Then working out how the catapult works and different ways to use it. He was also focused on applying sticky bits more accurately than he's done in the past. The rest of that particular kit  will likely remain untouched until he suddenly has a question that the kit answers. I've learnt over the years and so our house has several of these types of kits and subscriptions that have been used, then the interest has been met and it's been dropped, until an interest is reignited for some reason. Remember, learning is cyclic. Children tend to set self-imposed objectives to their learning and once that is met, they are satisfied to move away to something else and then at some point, a new objective might be explored with deeper learning needed on top of what was explored last time and round we go! When a resource is no longer being used, it could be that the resource doesn't meet the need or it could be that it is a brilliant resource and the need has been met, for now.

You had visions of you and your child excitedly exploring resources with enthusiasm and joy. But right now, instead it feels like your child will never show an interest in anything you consider educational ever again. Maybe everything you suggest is met with resistance.  Repeat that small sentence above because the crux of the issue is usually our own stuff. I know, it sucks! But as I've said before I truly believe deschooling is more about parents than kids.

Often, we are failing to see the learning that is right in front of us because we've got ourselves in a pickle of what we think is educational vs non educational. You see it's pretty rare for children to not show any interest in anything at all. But it's much less rare for us parents to place judgement on those interests and end up not seeing them as worthwhile, so we don't engage relating to those things and instead wait to see an interest we do think is worthy of exploring. And boom! Suddenly we notice our child showing a slight interest in something we consciously or unconsciously feel is worthwhile and we grab it by the horns and over enthusiastically engage. We research all the things, we download, buy, find every resource we can on it and then present it all to our children with an excited flourish only to be met with disdain. Maybe we download a twinkl project on the ISS and print all the things out, do all the cut outs, prep all the things ready for the children to come down the next morning full of surprise and excitement...can you tell I've been here with you? Instead, you are met with utter disappointment and disinterested grumpy kids who don't understand how you got here from them mentioning they watched a YouTube video on an egg toss in space...On reflection, you also begin to wonder how you got here when you've been home educating for nearly a decade and know your children don't engage in learning in this way...Sorry, enough about me! Basically, over enthusiastic engagement is the surest way to turn your children away from an interest and is also the best way to ensure your kids stop sharing their interests with you, which can lead to some really tough home education because we already know that kids learn best and most comprehensively when following their interests. So, what can you do instead? Firstly, notice what your children are already interested in and begin to show curiosity in that. Withhold judgement on whether you feel it's educational or not. Ask questions, learn more about the interest yourself, see if they would let you join them in that interest, encourage deep dives and long conversations (or info dumping as is the love language of our home) but do not suggest other resources or educational resources to expand it unless they directly ask you for input. Trust that by meeting them where they are at, you will learn more about them, how they learn, how they engage with the world and the resources they use, than you ever could imagine. Over time your children will begin to trust that they can share their interests with you, without you turning it into something else. They will feel more able to show you exactly how much learning is occurring already, because they are natural learners and in doing so, you will be able to see that they are learning and growing and expanding . You may even notice that you can be trusted to give your input, suggestions or ideas and they will be heard with excitement and interest because your child knows you just want to help them do more of the thing they are interested in, rather than turning it into something you value more.

*Me time*

Whether you are brand new to the concept of home education or old hat, it really is a life altering, all-encompassing journey so how do you find the balance? How do you let go of the expectations you have of what you think home ed should look like? How do you settle into the reality of it? And how do you maintain your sovereignty as adult human beings with needs and wants, when so much of your days are focused on your children? I'm not going to sit here and say it's easy because it's not, but it is essential for long term balance and success. Let me introduce you to the circles of life. We are going to look at who belongs where in your circles of life to help you draw clearer boundaries. So, grab a piece of paper and draw a small circle. Inside that circle is you. That's it, only you. Why don't you draw a little doodle of yourself? Now draw another slightly larger circle around the first. Add in anyone who lives in your home, any partners, family members who live in your home, your children, pets. This is your family unit. You and your immediate family. This is the top priority and who we will explore first.

As parents we often put our needs last, but not for this little exercise. So, starting with you: what do you need on a daily basis to feel balanced and healthy? What is the minimum? What is the minimum you need on a daily basis? Is it realistic? Is it possible right now or something to work towards? Whatever it is, it's doable if you and your family work towards it. For me, the minimum I need is sleep, some quiet time to myself in the morning and space to read with a cup of tea before bed. That's the minimum because as long as I have been able to read, sleep and had a little time to wake up without demands placed on me, the rest of my needs tend to slot in pretty well. These are non-negotiable. By non-negotiable I mean that they will happen daily because I make sure they happen. When the children were younger, this meant needing to wake earlier to ensure my morning time, as it was unreasonable to expect my very young children to not need me first thing. As the children grew, it meant getting into bed before the older children did so I could read my book. It has happened over time, with patience and realistic expectations. I do have a slightly unique view though as for the first 5 or 6 years of my 3rd child's life, I learnt if I needed to sleep, I had to do it anywhere and everywhere due to his medical needs and when you are constantly surrounded by medical staff, you learn how precious those moments to yourself with a cuppa really are too. These minimum non negotiables allow me to be the version of a parent and partner I want and need to be for my family. Think about your minimums and how you could make them work.

Now, the next circle out from you is your family. What are the minimums they each need daily? How do those interact with other people's needs? How can everyone learn to respect and appreciate others' needs in the home? At a minimum my husband needs to get ready for work before anyone else is up and he needs half an hour to himself when he gets in from work. At a minimum my youngest needs lots of space to talk things through and his dad to read him a story every night. One of the other children needs time alone to self-regulate when they come in from being out, safe foods to reach for and low demands. Another needs regular connection and discussion along with a specific bedtime routine. These are minimum non-negotiables for each person so everyone can have their minimum needs met. How does it work? My husband gets up early to get ready for work and is usually gone by 6.30am. I then get up and have a cuppa and some time to myself. If any of the children get up earlier than usual, they respect that it's my time, so they are quiet and find something to do away from mum. If a sibling needs time alone to regulate, they head upstairs, if there is someone in the space they need, they explain they need to be alone and the other person respects that and leaves. In that case the one leaving might head into my bedroom instead to chill. When the youngest needs time and space to talk something through, we explain that and ask for a little time. If dad is in later than planned, the youngest stays up longer until dad has had his half an hour so then they can enjoy reading together in bed. The needs are specific and non-negotiable so the plan around them is adjustable and fluid to ensure they can happen. It's taken years of consistent collaboration and adjusting and learning together, to get to a place where it can work and yes, even then stuff goes wrong and our home is naturally chaotic and loud and well, a lot. But these minimum non-negotiables help keep us all sane and respectful of each other, because we work together as a team and understand why we each need the things we do. Outside of these 2 circles are numerous others. The closer to your family unit, the more influence and energy and closeness. So, in the next circle out for us are other family members and very close friends. Next one out is people we know fairly well such as fewer close friends and family or people who have some kind of involvement with our family such as scout leaders, our doctor, the physio etc. Next one out, acquaintances, etc. The rest of the space around our circles of life is strangers. People who pass us in the street or who tut at my child flapping in Tesco. Depending on your circumstances the local authority will either sit in the space outside of your circles or maybe the furthest circle out. The closer to your inner family unit, the more influence and involvement they are likely to have and vice versa. The further away, the less influence and involvement. By clearly visualising on paper where your boundaries sit and who you feel belongs where, you are better able to approach your priorities for home ed and your family. We all care what people think or others' expectations, but this exercise can help you to see whether they really do need to make as much of an impact or not. Give it a try!

# When home ed is a struggle

Home Education sounds wonderful right? It drums up images of close knit, happy, content families out in the fresh air with children engaged in everything the parent puts in front of their eager little munchkins and I assure you, there are times that match that description beautifully but just as with any other family, home educated children are children and will behave exactly as children should. By that I mean there will be push back, challenges, difficulties, and struggles. I have the benefit of having had a foot in several worlds when it comes to education. I've had children who have been to school and become home educated, children who have returned to school after a period of home education, children who have never been to school and children who have home educated through teenhood and moved into formal further education. Through it all, the one thing I can say for sure is that regardless of how your child receives an education, they will still be children and those children will still grow into teenagers and young adults. That will still be challenging and chaotic and beautiful and rewarding and sometimes (often) exhausting! So, what do you do when it feels like home education is falling apart?

Children's drive for autonomy is hardwired (some more strongly than others) whether home educated or in school. That difficult stuff- the challenges, the non-engagement, the struggles, and pushback is all part of a child finding their own place in the world, what they stand for and who they are, and that is difficult to do when a large amount of your autonomy is taken away via rigid structures and other people's versions of what they feel is best for you. When a child leaves school education to become home educated that freedom from those structures can feel amazing, overwhelming or both! You might have a child who wants you to set things up like it was at school, and you are feeling like the best home edder ever, only for that child to then refuse to engage a few weeks or months down the line. You might have a view that learning needs to be at certain times and your child might be wanting to do anything but! You might have a child who is resistant to anything and everything remotely educational and wants to just sleep and watch TV or play video games. You might have a child who is overwhelmed by the choices now available to them and so simply can't engage in anything at all. You might have a child who is finally able to study deeply in academics they didn't have an option to study in school but won't engage in anything else that you feel is needed. These and more, are all really normal responses to becoming home educated and they also happen throughout your child's home ed journey too! But the benefit of home education is that your child's drive for autonomy can be nurtured, encouraged, and celebrated! When parents hear the words child and autonomy put together it often conjures up images of feral, wild, unwashed children, eating a diet of pure sugar, running rings around their parents. But supporting autonomy is not permissive or uninvolved parenting and it's certainly not uninvolved education either. When something doesn't feel like it's working for whatever reason, it's time for us as facilitators and parents to model our problem-solving skills and deepen our relationship with our child. Because in home ed, learning doesn't have to be prescriptive, and we can change and flow if and when needed! In our house we use collaborative proactive solutions and believe that everyone does well if they can. This is from Ross Greene - The explosive child. If they can't, there is a problem that needs attention, care, compassion, and collaboration. The best sentence I've ever seen via the CPS model is 'I've noticed 'xyz' what's up with that?'

## For example

My teen and I chatted a while back and together decided he would work through functional skills for English and maths. He had good reasons for wanting to do them but also had concerns about struggling with it as it's more formal and we haven't generally done formal learning as we are conversational learners. Together we decided he would work through the Functional Skills 1 study books, but he then struggled to pick them up. We had a chat about this where I explained I had noticed him struggling to do the books we set up and asked him what he feels is going on. The aim of the chat wasn't to get him to do what I want, but to find out what's really going on for him and then together come up with new plans and ideas that work for him and me. Sometimes the best plan might mean dropping the thing for now and focusing on other things too! My son explained that they are really boring and schooly and that he doesn't like being left to do them on his own so was struggling to pick them up. I had expected him to say they are boring and schooly because I totally agree (And would have understood even if I didn't agree) but the thing that struck me was him saying about being left to do them alone. I relayed to him what I had heard, and he explained more deeply that he wants to do functional skills as he feels they will provide options further down the line but that doing something boring on your own makes it even harder. I asked him what he felt might make that easier and he came up with a few brilliant solutions. Only needing to focus on one question in each book on the days he's doing them. Mum sitting with him and talking through the question together. Chatting together about how we would use that scenario in our daily lives so he could really get the point of it. Having snacks and siblings being elsewhere so he can focus and gaming time afterwards. His solutions were really good, and we implemented all of them. If he couldn't see any solutions, we would have dropped the books for now and focused on something else but with his concerns addressed and working on solutions together we found a way that works for us both.

Nowadays my kids come to me a lot with solutions to things I hadn't even realised were a problem yet, because they know I respect their autonomy, they know we can discuss anything without judgement and that together we can collaborate to find ways to work on stuff. Essentially, they know I'm on their side and that I will listen carefully and work together with them to help things work better and most importantly, they know that I expect them to be challenging, to push back and to be exhausting because those things are essential to growing up and becoming the independent, autonomous, self-governing adults they will become. So, what do we do when things aren't working? We reconnect, reassess and most importantly, know it's okay to change things up, or even drop them completely.

With all of that said, It is really important to understand that home ed won't work out for everyone, just like school won't work for everyone. It is no failure on anyone's part if after giving home ed a really solid try, it's just not working out and there are lots of reasons out of a parents control, why children may need to return to school however, it's important to remember a few points regarding the things we can influence. Many of us try the school system for a good few years before opting out and home ed needs to be given the same opportunity too. Many of us opt to home-ed for really significant and difficult reasons, if those reasons have disappeared or been healed through home ed, it means it's working, not that school will necessarily work now. The social scene of schooling is pre-arranged and organised. It's easier. Parents and children meet via the act of attending the same place on a daily basis at the same time. Home ed and life in general works completely differently and takes time and effort to find the people you all jive with. Way more time and effort than was probably expected but just because it's not the same doesn't mean it doesn't work. All of these things take time. They take weeks, months, years. Home ed won't work for everyone but it does deserve the best chance possible to see if it could.

Common reasons why home ed doesn't quite work out.

First let's explore some of the situations that make home ed really difficult regardless of how much you might want it to work.

## Finances

Finances are a very real and important thing to consider with home education. For many families home ed can mean one parent giving up work resulting in a significant loss of income. For other families it can mean both parents adjusting their hours meaning less money all round. For others it might mean juggling work and home ed as a single parent or having to give up paid work to support your child at home. While home education can be done on a low budget, there is usually a financial sacrifice somewhere and I don't know if you've noticed, but making ends meet has never been harder for the majority of people in our country. Sometimes no matter how much you want to continue home education, you simply aren't able to financially. It might be a more general issue like not being able to provide the opportunities or resources you want to, or as serious as the reality of keeping a roof over your head. Sometimes life really is just utterly unfair. What I will say is it's important to check you are getting any and all financial support that you are entitled to as a parent. Child benefit, universal credit, disability living allowance, carers allowance, and other financial support is available to those who need it regardless of where a child is educated. Please do apply for these if you are entitled as it can make a difference.

## Burn out.

Home ed can be really intense. You are spending more time with your children than ever before and while that can be wonderful, it can also be utterly exhausting especially if your child has experienced trauma in the school environment or is disabled. Not having family nearby to provide help and support, being your child's safe space to feel regulated, safe, and secure and being unable to have time to yourself can lead to serious burnout. Add sleep deprivation into the mix and it's a recipe for a really unwell parent. As someone with chronic illnesses and neurodivergent needs it is a constant juggling act to ensure that my children's needs are met, but also my own, so that I don't become unwell. Developing a network of support has been essential for me, but in reality, not everyone has access to that, especially single parents. Even when my child was unable to be away from me, I had friends and family who were a phone call away, or able to come and cook dinner, or have the other children for a while or just helped take any of the load that was able to be taken. There are still times that I am unwell and then my husband needs to take time off and become me for a few days, but it has definitely improved as the children have gotten older. But I really had to explore all the options available and find ways to make it work for us all. In some cases, no matter what you try, you simply are not in a position to find a way through. Your children need you to be able to be there to support them and if not home edding makes it possible for you to do that better, that's just how it needs to be. I know it's rarely that simple when you have complex children who cannot get their needs met in a school, but please know there is absolutely nothing wrong with needing to look after you.

## Unhealed pain

When you didn't elect to home educate as a first or even 3rd choice, it can be really hard. Those of us who came to home education via feeling forced into a corner can really struggle to adjust. You might be angry, exhausted, and traumatised from trying everything to help your child attend school and it not working out. You may be grieving the life you expected. All of this is a normal reaction to your life being turned upside down and so it is all a process. By all means write the complaints, take on the government, push all that rage into whatever medium you need. But you will need to find a way to let go and move forward before it turns into resentment, because home educating in an energy of resentment is not going to help any of you. Give yourself the time to begin to heal. Give yourself the opportunity to talk it out with friends, family, therapists. It's a slow process but it's essential so you can move forward into a space of embracing home education instead of looking backwards and the school system that failed your child. Reluctant home education is a really challenging space to be in, but most of us can move through it with time and kindness to ourselves.

Now let's look at some of the more common factors that can cause home ed to not work out, but that can be easier to work through. Most of them require a change of approach on the parents' side, not the children.

## Deschooling

I need to be super honest here, one of the top things I see is that parents haven't been able to take the time to deschool themselves. Without deschooling, parents will struggle to see the plethora of learning opportunities available that exist outside of the school environment and so they will end up judging their home ed against school-based standards and expectations. The child is often refusing to engage in the work set by the parent, or rushing through it to be able to move onto something they enjoy. The parents feel at a loss. They feel disrespected, overwhelmed, and panicked that they are failing their child. All of this can genuinely be supported with a big old dose of back to basics and deschooling.

## Confidence

Many parents feel confident in supporting learning in a younger child but as the child gets older, parents often feel overwhelmed and unable to meet their child's growing needs, especially if their child's abilities feel like they are higher than the parent or the parent is struggling to understand the content of the education they are trying to help their children with. The question I often ask these parents is whether they want to put their children through the same school system that left them feeling as lacking in education as they currently feel. Because feeling a bit out of your depth is normal in this experience, but feeling like you cannot support your children to learn, because of the schooling you received is just heartbreaking. The thing we need to remember is that children are natural learners and as home ed parents, we do not need to be their teacher. What they need is a partner, a cheerleader, a facilitator. They need a parent who can model that it's natural to not know everything and to then work together to find the answers. They need a parent who can say 'I don't know, let's find out'. They don't need you to have the answers, they need you to support them in finding their own answers.

## Inflexible mindset

When we become home educators, we ~~adds~~ ~~lea~~
view of how it's going to work. What t
happen and how. We may have a view of w...
important and tailor the education to that. Our chilu...
come along and complicate things by making it clear t.
the way we parents want to do it won't work. This doesn
mean home education doesn't work, it just means that the
way that has been tried so far, hasn't worked well. When we
are unable to adapt and be flexible with our approach it can
lead to some big problems. Reassessing and being open to
letting your child tell you what's working and what isn't, is
key.

## Own learning

Us parents are often our own worst critics and so we
naturally place higher expectations on ourselves to have all
the answers. We only know what we know but with home
education itself being really time consuming, it can be hard
to find the time to gain a deeper understanding as to what
learning actually is and to explore the various types of
learning too. You might be aware that something doesn't
seem to be working well, but because you don't have the
time to research anything else, you just double down on
what you do know. Recognising that home ed provision
develops and grows over time is essential. Finding even 10
minutes a day to read a book or watch a video relating to
learning styles, approaches, child development etc is a must.
Even if that time is spent simply scrolling on home ed
support groups and picking a post to read through, it all

up. Please stop putting a time limit on your own
ning journey and give your own home education the
he and space it needs to grow.

## Lack of social opportunities

As a home educator who supports other home educators a
common reason families come to me with concerns and
thoughts of returning to school is socialisation. They are
worried that their child isn't seeing other people enough.
Their child wants to see the same people every day outside
of the family circle. Their child prefers online socialising and
parents don't feel this is enough. The parents feel there isn't
enough activity in their community. The thing with social
opportunities is that home educators have to be proactive
and committed to finding ways to make it work. Home ed is
not the same as school and events are not necessarily all set
up ready for you to pick and choose. If there isn't something
in your area, you set it up. If your child wants more
opportunities, you need to find ways to get that happening.
But you both also need to adjust your expectations as
expecting home ed to look like school is only going to make
things difficult. Understanding your child's personality is key
as we are all different. Some children like to be out daily
spending time with others. Some prefer their own company
or a more indirect way of spending time with others. It takes
time to find your feet and find your people. What I will say is
that almost every area has home educators. Every LA area
does. And you'll be amazed how many families there actually
are in your area once you find them. If after trying
everything, your child wants to return to school for the social
element, it's important to recognise that alongside that will

be all the other stuff they will be expected to commit to as well. Remember, you don't go to school to socialise!

**Time**

The biggest factor that occurs in all of these is time. One of the first questions asked of a home educator who feels home ed isn't working is "How long have you been home educating?" This is because starting home education is one of the biggest and discombobulating experiences for both you and your child and it really does take time to settle into it. It takes time to find your feet. Time to find styles that work. Time for a style to bed in to see if it works. Time to find groups and events and return over time to see how it feels. It takes time to learn more about how your child learns best, time to heal from any difficulties. It takes time to develop your provision. Time to drop into a new rhythm. It all takes time and sadly, time is the one thing that many families don't give themselves enough of. Anything new takes time to apply and when you are then also trying to unpick your own understanding of learning and education, learning the EHE guidelines, learning so many new things, it takes even more time. The beauty of home education is that it gives you and your child the time back, to be able to find your way. Give it time.

*Confession time!*

I don't think it matters how long you've been home educating; you still have moments where you question it all. Personally, I tend to have 2 major wobbles a year, usually around February and September. The September wobble makes sense with the start of the academic school year, pictures of people's children all off to school in their fresh and crisp uniforms but I am yet to understand the February wobble, even after several years! What's a wobble? Well for me it's a moment where I begin to compare home education to school, I begin to feel we aren't doing enough or that the kids should be doing some other form of home education. I've come to see these moments as great opportunities to reflect and check in, but it's taken years to recognise them and reframe them in that way!

And sometimes life throws you a curveball. One year, September came and went and there was not a wobble in sight. In hindsight I now know that was because I was too busy to notice. For a second, I thought "Yes! I've cracked it! I'm finally just doing my thing and not worrying at all" oh how I am laughing about that now. Because the wobble of course reared its head with a dramatic flourish in the November instead. It was so simple. A school parent friend of mine noted that my child would be in a specific year group now if he was in school. It was a completely innocent comment. But alas, cue a total midlife, what the hell am I doing, crisis.

It's important to note that wobbles are normal, and I would be more worried if I didn't have them. As autonomous self-directed home edders it's even more important to know where you've been, where you are at and where you are heading because you often don't have the same checks and measures that structured, or semi structured approaches have via academic curriculums studied or workbooks/courses completed. So, when I have wobbles, I grab my phone and look at the pictures we take on an almost daily basis. I work from today backwards until I frankly feel overwhelmed by how much we've done together as a family over time. Because that's the thing with home education, and education in general- it happens over time like a beautiful painting. If you were to look at a painting in the beginning stages, it may just look like a few non-descript colours on a canvas. Over time, the layers of the background, the foreground, the details, and the finer points appear, and home education is the same. If you were to view it in just one day and judge the education by that one snapshot, well it would be easy to believe you were failing. But it's not one day. It's layer upon layer of days and weeks and months and years creating this beautiful masterpiece of learning and growing and developing. Each piece builds upon the next to create new meaning, new understanding, and new application. Another thing I do when in wobble mode is to take it as an opportunity to seek out new ideas, new resources, and to check in with the children's constantly growing interests. This time around we've discovered some new resources to try, it doesn't mean we will definitely use these resources, but they are itching my scratch during a wobble and the children are loving the new challenge they pose right now.

The children know when I'm having a wobble as I'm honest about it. They know it's normal and they know it's an opportunity to reflect together, see what's working well, what they've lost interest in and what they are currently wanting to explore. They were a bit disappointed that there are no pretty, laminated timetables to laugh at that time round though! For me, what's important is the recognition that learning is cyclic and seasonal. It spirals and weaves in and out of interests and time and space and what is of focus in spring and summer may be left by the wayside in autumn and winter only to be rediscovered again the following year. And so, around we all weave, through the wobbles that provide fresh thoughts and ideas, and we can smile, knowing all is as it should be. Well, until next time anyway!

*Time for a Breather!*

Home Education is hard, and it can be even harder when you are having a wobble, or your circumstances have changed.

Do you have a plan for when things like this crop up?

We call ours the back-to-basics plan where we get together and work out what is absolutely necessary, what is needed and what is wanted in an ideal situation.

Could you draw up something similar?

Think of it like an emergency plan, a wobble plan, a crisis plan so that you can stay grounded and work as a team to work through the challenge.

# Myths and Misconceptions

Part of the joy of home ed is learning about our own preconceived ideas and unpicking them. There is of course a whole chapter in the book dedicated to exactly that; Deschooling! But I wanted to have a closer look at some of the myths and misconceptions that come up a lot in the home ed arena specifically as these are classic expectations vs reality but usually, they are more about the perceptions of others, rather than about home edders themselves.

*Home Education happens at home.*

The idea that home ed happens at home is a huge misconception and drives many of the fear-based rhetoric you read in newspapers around home education too. When people think of home education, they might imagine the child sitting at a table with workbooks, pen and paper and their parents teaching them a subject. If they have succumbed to the headlines, they might even imagine a Harry Potter style situation with the child locked under the stairs by evil parents denying the child an education or providing nothing at all! In truth, a home educating home looks pretty much the same as other family homes, only we have more laminators and craft supplies and definitely less money!

School children leave their home early in the morning and are dropped off at school, where they typically spend around 6 hours on the school premises before returning home again. So, what do home educators do while school children are in school buildings getting an education? Well, here's a little secret for you, they are probably not at home! Many home edders use this opportunity to take their education out into the world outside of the home while other children are in school. It's one of the perks of home ed I could not do without nowadays, but it wasn't always like this.

*Confession time*

One of the things that has taken me a long time to get used to, is how different our lives look as home edders. When my older children were in school our days looked very similar to everyone else. Get up, struggle to get the kids to school, never be able to find that one shoe, deal with the screaming heartbroken 6-year-old being yanked off my leg and then get home and collapse in an emotional heap before getting on with my day with the baby. The afternoon was made up of collecting the children, being the mum, every teacher needed to talk to after school each day, having a cry in the car and then home for dinner, baths, bed, and a large glass of something to take the edge off before doing it all again. I dreaded the holidays and weekends knowing I would need to find ways to occupy and entertain the children, especially with everywhere being so busy and my kids not being able to cope with that. I was one of those parents that celebrated the countdown of back to school after the 6 weeks holidays and couldn't wait to give the kids back to someone else to deal with. But that's just how life goes right? As a parent of children in school you have to accept that kids won't want to go to school, but hey, we all have to do things we don't want to do. You accept that school is best. You accept that it's normal to have to drag them to school and you accept that it's a mark of parental community to need a strong drink to see you through it all.

My word, I was deep into that conditioning! Nowadays I don't recognise the mum I once was because I actually like my children now! I have to say that when we became home ed, a lot of the friends I had slowly slipped away. We just didn't have anything much in common to talk about anymore because our entire friendships had been made up of supporting each other over how hard this parenting stuff is. That is not to say home education is not hard, it's just a very different kind of experience. I'm not struggling to get my kids up at ridiculous times in the morning. I'm not dealing with arbitrary rules on clothing choice and hair styles. I'm not dealing with anxious, upset, struggling children and I don't need alcohol to make it all okay at the end of the day. Instead, the friends I have now are mainly fellow home educators or people I have something unrelated to children in common with!

While friends with school kids are making weekend plans, we are snuggling down for a weekend of homely board games, films, and food. While friends with school kids are driving round everywhere for after school activities, our evenings are spent at home, chatting, cooking, learning. While friends with school kids are trying to sort plans for the holidays to occupy and entertain, we are hibernating and seeing a select few friends in each other's homes to avoid the summer mayhem.

You see, while school children are at school, we are out instead. We are out at the parks, the library, home ed groups, museums. We are out on day trips and doing our shopping and enjoying the local area. Those after school clubs? We are doing those during the day instead so naturally, we are home when they aren't and we are out, when they are in school.

The half terms and weekends and holidays have become times to rest and hibernate and enjoy quietly, while the rest of the children in the country are out letting off steam! And then, as they return to the classrooms, we venture back out and reclaim the wonderful world made available for home educators. Our worlds are different. Our lives are different. But the one thing I know for sure, is that we are each doing the best with what we've got. When I was a school mum, I could never have imagined a world where my days weren't made up of struggle and stress and anxiety, it was the parenting badge I wore with pride and yet here I am, nearly a decade later enjoying my days with the kids, and the kids enjoying their days 24/7.

This is the thing with misconceptions and misinformation. Unless you are given the facts alongside the opinion, it's hard to know what to believe and this is something that irritates me no end with the media. The facts are that home educators are not required to do lots of things we might usually associate with school and there is absolutely nothing wrong with that. Home education is legal and how we do it is up to the parents, providing it takes up a significant proportion of the child's time, does what it sets out to do and is suited to the child's age, aptitude, ability, and any specific needs.

For example, while children attending school normally have about five hours of tuition a day for 190 days a year, spread over about 38 weeks, home education does not have to mirror this. Home educating parents are not required to have a timetable, to have set hours during which education will take place and they are not required to observe school hours, days, or terms. So, if your child doesn't sleep at night and midnight is their best time to learn, that's okay! (Although not necessarily so great for the parents) but also if you and your child want to observe school terms that's okay too. You just don't have to.

You might also be surprised to learn that there are no legal requirements for home edders to have any specific qualifications, or have a home equipped to any particular standard. Home edders don't have to aim for their child to do any specific qualifications such as GCSEs or teach the National Curriculum. Home edders don't need to provide a 'broad and balanced' curriculum or make detailed lesson plans or give formal lessons and home edders do not legally need to match school-based, age-specific standards.

This means that home educators have the freedom to support their child's learning in whatever ways are best for their family and at whatever time is best too. For us, we tend to have a daily and weekly rhythm that works. We have chilled early mornings catching up on projects (including me) and then early afternoons spent out in the community at events, trips, meet ups and activities. We aim to be home by around 3ish before places become busier with children leaving school and then evenings are spent together playing games, reading, watching movies, or chatting together. Learning is happening during all of these time periods as we do not separate education away from daily life. So again, home education happens at home? Sometimes yes, but far less than you presume and in very different ways to how you might imagine!

**Parents aren't teachers, so they aren't qualified to teach their children.**

One of the most common questions you will likely be asked by an interested member of the public, when they realise you home educate, will be something along the lines of "oh are you a teacher?". And guess what? Whether you are or not makes very little difference in your ability to home educate. There are indeed lots of teachers, ex teachers, higher education lecturers, child development professionals, social workers and child related professionals that home educate and there are many more who are not. This is because you do not need to be qualified in anything to be a home educator. Home education and mass schooling are two entirely different beasts.

A teacher is taught how to provide instruction to a large class of children. They are taught methods and techniques for crowd management. They are taught the basics of child development, and this may differ from course to course depending on the theory most popular at the time. They are taught about what England feels children should be expected to learn at different age points and how to deliver that, how to assess that, how to manage that, as well as behaviour management. These are all super important skills for teaching in a classroom and there are many transferable skills into various other areas of employment. But there is a surprisingly small amount of skills that transfer to home educating your own child because home ed is about fitting the education to the child, rather than the child to the education.

If anything, working in teacher related areas can actually make it harder to step into the wide and varied ways home ed can happen because you've been trained to see education in a specific way. This doesn't mean the qualifications and experiences aren't valid and respected, it just means they don't necessarily apply to how home education works in practice.

As parents, we are experts in our children and so having teacher qualifications doesn't make someone any more of an expert in home education than another. Now, from a societal perspective I am sure that if you have teaching or child related qualifications, local authorities worry less about your home education but again, this has nothing to do with home ed itself and everything to do with what we've been schooled to believe about what education looks like. A parent is the person best placed to understand their child's educational needs and abilities because it is the parent that is the one with those children every single day. That parent having teaching qualifications just enables them to recognise how different home ed is, to anything they've done before!

You don't need to have passed your own GCSEs to home ed your own children. You don't need to have a degree or have been to college. You don't need to have any specific skills at all. You know what you do need? Time, energy and commitment to your child and their learning journey. If you don't know something, work alongside your child to work it out together. If you struggle with a particular area of learning, ask for support from someone who doesn't. If you have family and friends who are skilled or experts in specific areas, Ask them to help out! Give your children the tools to take charge of their own learning and then facilitate that by providing the resources they need. It's not all about you and your skills, it's about your willingness to help your child get where they want to go.

Okay, let's get to grips with a few of the myths that remain rampant despite home education becoming more known and mainstream than ever before. First off, the classic:

*Home Education is illegal.*

This myth is one that I knew wasn't true. Logically it couldn't have been as I knew of families that were home educated and yet, I really did doubt my logic several times anyway! In truth, home education is of equal legal standing as a schooled education. This is via those two little words in section 7 of the education act 1996 that state 'or otherwise'. It is parents who are responsible for ensuring their children receive a suitable education but not many of us know this, until we come up against issues that require us to know. It doesn't help that home education has different legal status in various countries. In Germany, Iran, Turkey, Croatia, Greece, Netherlands, Spain, and Sweden home education is illegal or virtually illegal. In other countries such as France, Thailand, Belgium, Russia, Denmark, Finland, Hungary, Italy etc, home ed may be allowed but is heavily regulated with permissions required and regular scrutiny expected. Home education is very common in the USA and Canada as well as Australia and New Zealand, but each state or area will have its own policies on how regulated home educators are. For example, in the USA, Oklahoma parents are reasonably free from state oversight, whereas in Ohio this is the opposite.

All this is basically to say that this myth is indeed a myth in regard to England, but I can understand why not many of us know the legal status of home education or the laws on our own parental duties.

*Home educated children lack social skills.*

This one is always a doozy. It harks back to the misconception above that has people believing that all home educated children are locked away at home, isolated from the world. As someone who has been to school, has had children in school, had them out of school and then back in again, I can say with certainty that if school is what teaches our younger generation social skills, we are in dire trouble. However, if we are looking for mass socialisation via indoctrination into a specific capitalist culture, school is definitely your best bet. It's also great for forcing neurodivergent people to appear more neurotypical simply through repeated exposure and bullying. Which is just what every neurodivergent person wants right? (And they say it's us ND people who are bad at sarcasm?)

There's often a misunderstanding between socialisation and socialising when it comes to home ed and while in truth it's not a big deal which we are talking about, it helps to know more about it. Socialisation is the act of learning to behave in the ways that are deemed acceptable in our society. This is the stuff official's worry about when it comes to home education. After all, how will these children be conditioned and made to comply with the way our society works if they don't go to school to learn it?! Won't somebody please think of the children! Pause for dramatic effect...Socialising on the other hand is the act of spending time in the company of others, usually friends, doing activities together for fun. In truth both social skills and socialising exist under the same umbrella of socialisation and all of it is important and interconnected for human development and growth but what strikes me as odd, is how deep our conditioning goes when it comes to seeing school as the primary way in which children develop social skills.

Children in school spend 6 hours a day in the company of people the exact same age as them. They are governed by arbitrary rules around time, clothing, and hairstyles. They are told what to think, when to eat and pee, what is worth learning about (and not) and that there are right and wrong answers to everything, based on whatever the curriculum aim is at the time. Then difficulties arise, punishment is the order of the day with little reconciliation practice.

There is nowhere in the world and no other age bracket in life, that this type of encompassing restriction to a person's own self exists. Well, there is one other place and that's prison. Worryingly, having had children in the current school system up until 2023, I think prisoners may still have more autonomy than school children and I don't say that lightly. Children who are given choice and have their autonomy respected are more engaged, less disruptive, and more self-motivated, they feel empowered in their learning and are provided with the skills they actually need to move into adult life. We know this because researchers have been publicly working out how child development works and how we can best educate children since the early 19th century. How those in charge have concluded that removing a child from that system is dangerous for social skills, astounds me. School teaches skills essential for coping and surviving in the school environment only. Not in wider society.

In contrast most home educators are well documented to be proactive and committed to giving their children access to a rich age range of people from different walks of life, where they can learn and explore in a variety of ways at a variety of times without restrictions on their own bodily autonomy. By ensuring their children have access to the wider community they learn important social skills and socialisation from being out in the real world, experiencing life as it truly exists, as opposed to the falsified clinical social environments that school's model. Home-ed children have the benefit of forming natural friendships that are based on shared interests and commonalities (like adults do) rather than on arbitrary rules around age and academic level and these friendships tend to span not only the local home education community, but wider society as a whole. (Like adults do)

I wonder whether the reason socialisation is bandied around as an issue for home education is because the majority of the research carried out consistently finds that home educated children not only have typically better academic achievements, but also possess a deeper and stronger range of beneficial social skills needed for adulthood. I don't have the answer to that, but it doesn't exactly paint a great picture of school being right for those particular skills does it. For research around this in the UK have a nose into Paula Rothermel, Harriet Pattison, Alan Thomas and Amber Fensham - Smith.

*Home educated children can't get qualifications / go to college / University.*

One of the most common myths I see is the idea that children who are home educated are school dropouts. Without school these children can't get any qualifications. They can't go to college or on to university and they will never amount to anything.

Sadly, it's a myth perpetuated and vocalised within schools constantly and families considering home education are often bombarded with  false information in a strange desperation to keep children enrolled. What's worse is that many teachers and school staff believe this as absolutely true. They are so deeply indoctrinated into the school way, that it completely escapes them that there is any other way to do it. My advice is to always take what schools say about home ed with a pinch of salt and a healthy dose of scepticism. They rarely understand the guidelines around home education let alone the intricacies of it so speak to the people who do know, home educators!

Home Educators do not legally have to take exams or participate in the certifications that schooled children do. This is not the same as saying they can't. In truth a large majority of home-ed teens do indeed participate in the taking of GCSEs and A levels as well as other certifications such as functional skills and vocational diplomas like BTECs. The difference is that families are free to choose which exams feel relevant or important and focus on those. Home educators fund all exams and certifications themselves and there is  no outside funding available, but families don't have to do 10 GCSEs in one go like within school. There is no minimum amount of GCSEs that must be taken, and they can also be spread  out across a number of years meaning there is significantly less pressure involved both psychologically and financially. There is also no minimum or maximum age that these can be taken either! The range of certifications available to home educators is far greater than a state curriculum allows, especially with access to iGCSEs too and with no compulsory core subjects, teens can focus on what they've collaboratively chosen is needed for where they want to head next.

What's also important to keep in mind is that of those GCSE age children in state school, 30% will fail to obtain a pass in English and maths simply by default anyway. This is because of the way exams are graded and the horrendous system of 'comparable outcomes'. This is not a new issue, or one brought about by the Pandemic, this is a simple fact of the current education system in England. The GCSE results in schools in 2019 (the last 'good' year pre pandemic) were that 35.6% of students failed to gain a standard pass in English or maths.   With around 600,000 students taking GCSEs each year, that equates to about 200,000 students who will be judged as not being able to meet the 'standard' pass after 12 years in school. Every year.

We don't have accurate data for how many home educators pass GCSEs, as their data gets mixed up with private candidates in general and we don't know exactly how many go on to college and university, but we do know that when they decide to do exams it's because they've been chosen. When they do go to university, it's because they are clear and focused on what they want to achieve. My eldest is one such example who after being unschooled from age 11, went to University a year early. There are many other examples of home educators who go on to further study and I'd recommend a deep dive into the HE Exams Wiki for more stories of success, as they have an entire section dedicated to the personal experiences of home educators. So yes, home educators do go on to gain qualifications, they do go on to college and they also go on to university too. There are home educators who successfully run their own businesses, who work in vocational arenas and so much more. The myth that home edders are dropouts is perpetuated by the simplistic view of school equalling the only way to get an education.

## Time for a breather and a quiz!

That was quite a few soap boxes to get through so well done!

Time for some loud music to shake off the rage and a strong cup of chamomile. There are of course lots of other myths and misconceptions around home education, but these were the main ones that I wish I had known the realities of.

Let's have a little end of chapter true or false quiz! (Groan)

Home Education must happen during school hours. (True / False)

You must hold a teaching qualification to home ed. (True / False)

Home Educated children don't have to do GCSEs. (True / False)

Home Education is legal in Spain. (True / False)

Parents are responsible for ensuring children receive an education. (True / False)

Home edders usually have poor social skills. (True / False)

Home educating families have to pay for exams themselves. (True / False)

Home educators can't go to university. (True / False)

## Reflection

What other myths can you think of? What kinds of questions have you been asked by others? Reflect on where those ideas or opinions really come from.

# Safeguarding

Safeguarding is never an easy discussion to have and always an emotive one. When it is mentioned in home education communities it often feels like there are two warring sides to choose from and no room for discussion. Side one says this, side two says that and the ever emotional and passionate debate continues. The truth is probably somewhere in between and far more nuanced, a nuance I'm going to attempt to show below. With a hand on my heart, I will likely do so with poor success as it feels impossible to encompass this conversation into one chapter of a book. Home educators are not a monolith, we are not a static group of people with set types of belief or view and no one person, group or organisation can speak for all home educators. We can only each speak for ourselves, which I will do below. My aim is to provide information to help demonstrate the complexity of safeguarding and home education as well as give space to discuss my own thoughts around this important subject. The issues and history of home education and safeguarding is complex, just as safeguarding children in general is complex. I do share some cases of harm and although they may be rare, they are also horrendous and have understandably been the cause of some of the distrust and animosity between those with a duty to keep children safe, the home ed community and the wider public.

Safeguarding is a word we hear a lot as parents and rightfully so. While its meaning is simple, its actions and methods of delivery vast. Safeguarding is essentially the act of protecting a person's right to live in safety, free from abuse, harm, or neglect. I don't know about you, but it feels like a no-brainer that we would want that for everyone. In particular we have a responsibility to safeguard all children and vulnerable adults who could be more easily affected by abuse, harm, or neglect. The primary responsibility for safeguarding a child falls to the child's parents and caregivers but every single person who comes into contact with that child will have a role to play in ensuring children are safe generally. There are also state services that have legal duties placed upon them to promote the wellbeing and safety of children too and in the UK these services have reactive duties to step in if there are potential risks of harm identified. Basically, this means that parents are presumed to be doing their duty to safeguard their children, unless information comes to light that this may not be the case.

Ensuring a healthy balance between the right to a family life, respecting parental responsibility, children's rights, and the state's duty to protect children, is a difficult one to apply at times. For example, article 8 of the Human Rights Act protects your right to respect for your family life and your home meaning you have the right to live your family life privately without government interference, however there are situations when the government can interfere with these rights such as when it comes to the rights and freedoms of other, such as children. Children have their own rights as the individual, sovereign human beings that they are and many of these are separate and distinct from being the child of a parent. Children do not belong to a parent; they are not property. Parents are legally and morally *responsible* for children and responsible for ensuring their child's rights. This distinction is important. Children have 54 specific articles via the CRC (United Nations Convention on the Rights of a Child) which specifically sets out the human rights of children and is the most widely adopted human rights treaty in history. We live in a country that ratified the UNCRC in 1991, meaning that adults and governments must work together to make sure the rights within the UNCRC are afforded to children. Respecting the rights of people to live free from government interference is important, but so are children's rights and so is the government's duty to ensure children can enjoy those rights. Like I said, it's all a fine balance.

When we think of safeguarding it is easy to jump straight to thoughts of horrendous abuse at the hands of evil parents or people in a position of trust, because these are often discussed more, it can feel like it's commonplace, but actually, these types of horrendous abuse are rare in terms of the population. If a person is determined to harm a child, they will find a way, regardless of the safeguarding measure we put in. But again, it's more nuanced than that. Promoting the welfare and safety of children is multifaceted, complex and the causes of children needing support are not always within a parent's abilities to change.

One such example is financial instability. On 23rd March 2023 the government announced its latest data on households with below average income for 2022. Child Poverty Action Groups' press release showed that 29% of children in the UK are living in poverty.[7] This is 29% of all children currently growing up in families who cannot afford the basics. That's around 4.2 million children. Many people presume these families are non-working but 71% of these children come from working families. Do you know what the top form of harm children experience is? It's neglect (and not necessarily wilful neglect). We already know that the socioeconomic factors of poverty, poor housing and deprivation are some of the highest risk factors involved in a child needing support, alongside domestic violence. After years of austerity and now a cost-of-living crisis, many of us are just a few bad months away from dropping below those poverty lines, if we aren't already there and with that comes stress, anxiety, mental health challenges or worse. Parents hold the ultimate responsibility of looking after their children and keeping them safe, but my word, that is a challenge in the current climate. It's not only a challenge for parents, but a monumental challenge for services who are meant to step in to support families when they need it. If a third of children need that support, how do you work out who needs it most? For children's services this comes in the form of assessing needs against a threshold of potential or current harm which is no easy task when so many children are not even having their most basic needs met because of societal situations that are not necessarily easily changed by the parent.

---

[7] Child poverty 2022 https://cpag.org.uk/news-blogs/news-listings/official-child-poverty-statistics-350000-more-children-poverty-and-numbers

The reason I am drawing attention to this one small element of the complexities is because there is often a focus in home ed safeguarding discussions around serious case reviews, deaths, or serious harms, when these are one part of the story. It's right that we speak about what happened to those children, but it must be done in a way that respects them and respects that those cases aren't the full story. Neglect is the most common form of abuse in our country and can have serious and long-lasting impacts on a person's life, yet sadly people rarely understand that their upbringing was neglectful, until they are adults.

An NSPCC study (Radford et al., 2011) found that around 1 in 10 children in the UK have been neglected and in 2020/21 the NSPCC's helpline responded to a total of 84,914 contacts from people who were concerned about a child's welfare. 12,833 contacts related to concerns about neglect, making it the 2nd most discussed concern and the most mentioned form of abuse.[8]

The Crime Survey for England and Wales (CSEW) estimated that 1 in 100 adults aged 18 to 74 years experienced physical neglect before the age of 16 years (481,000 people); this includes not being taken care of or not having enough food, shelter, or clothing, but it does not cover all types of neglect.[9] Around half of adults (52%) who experienced abuse before the age of 16 years also

---

[8] NSPCC statistics briefing: Neglect 2021
[9] ONS 2019
https://www.ons.gov.uk/peoplepopulationandcommunity/crimeand justice/articles/childneglectinenglandandwales/yearendingmarch20 19

experienced domestic abuse later in life, compared with 13% of those who did not experience abuse before the age of 16 years.[10]

All forms of abuse and harm to children is devastating and for those still alive today, the impacts are far reaching. There of course continues to be far too many cases of serious harm. In 2021 the child safeguarding practice review panel provided their annual report. In it 723 children were known to have been affected by a serious incident. 398 of these children were directly affected and 325 children were indirectly affected (meaning for example that they witnessed the incident or were affected by the incident as a family member). 156 of the children directly affected, sadly died and 242 suffered serious harm. 33.2% of these children were open to children's social care and 66.8% were previously known to children's social care. Of the 398 children directly involved in a serious incident, 11.1% were on a Child Protection Plan at the time and 56.8% had been on a Child protection plan at least once before. The two prominent age groups when harm happened to these children were under 1 years old at 32% and between 11 -15 at 26%. The following issues were identified by safeguarding partners in rapid reviews: Weak risk assessment and decision making in 70.1% of cases, Lack of frequency and quality of supervision by services in 67.3% of cases, Poor escalation of concerns in 63.6% of cases, Lack of professional curiosity in 72.9% of cases and lack of

---

[10] ONS 2020
https://www.ons.gov.uk/peoplepopulationandcommunity/crimeand justice/bulletins/childabuseinenglandandwales/march2020

coordination or handover between services in 56.5% of cases.[11]

In the same year of 2021 there were 597,760 referrals to children's social care and a further 135,850 re-referrals. (Meaning a child was referred back to the service within those 12 months). 50,010 of these referrals resulted in a child being placed on a child protection plan. To put all of these figures into context there were around 12 million children living in England in 2021, and just under 3% of those children were in the social care system at any one time[12]. These figures worry me as even if all of those 600,000 children were also identified as being in poverty (which I doubt is the case) that's less than 15% of them (4.2 million children). Again, the safeguarding of children is significantly complex, multifaceted, and rarely as simple as the media, home educators or the state like to make out.

One huge issue I see, is that social care services are underfunded, understaffed, and overworked. I personally know several social workers and while they genuinely love their job and went into it to help and support families, they have the same fears as anyone else. What if they fail to spot an issue? What if one of the children they are charged with supporting becomes another heartbreaking statistic on the

---

[11] Child safeguarding practice panel review
https://www.gov.uk/government/publications/child-safeguarding-practice-review-panel-annual-report-2021
[12] Children's social care data 2021
https://www.gov.uk/government/statistics/childrens-social-care-data-in-england-2021

government's website? What if they could have done more? The underfunding of social care services and the crises caused by austerity and the pandemic has directly led to other services being tasked with firefighting for families not caught by the children's social care net. Services such as teaching and local authority employees not within the social care sector, have had their responsibilities subtly amended to fill the gap, with varying success. Safeguarding training is provided but this is very hit and miss. I've completed the safeguarding training myself and I can unequivocally state that social workers have degrees in this stuff for good reason. Teachers, head teachers and LA staff are not social workers but when enhanced safeguarding is pushed onto them, they take on responsibilities they aren't necessarily qualified to hold or action. In short, the whole system is a mess but doing its best.

*What does any of this have to do with home education?*

Home educated children are as entitled to safeguarding measures as any other child. Home education is not a risk factor for harm and not an automatic safeguarding concern in and of itself. But again, it's more complex than that. Depending on the child's circumstances it can be a factor that when considered in a wider frame, becomes a red flag. In some cases, this can be the correct action, which I discuss further down. In other cases, it's not. For example, despite home education being of equal legal standing, people who work with children are not trained sufficiently to understand what home education is. We continue to see doctors, teachers, dentists, opticians, and social workers who do not even know that home education is legal in

England, let alone that it's of equal legal standing to a school education. We continue to see head teachers who overstep their responsibilities to the extent of refusing deregistration of children because they feel they know what's best for a child and presume their views supersede a parent's legal responsibility. Sadly, there remains a view that deregistering or not opting for school is nefarious and without proper training or even knowledge of the guidelines and law around home education, we will continue to fight that battle.

Lack of training around it is understandable though as until recently home education was a fairly uncommon course of action for parents and mainly one enjoyed by philosophical home educators. However, it has been steadily rising year on year, with a sharp rise during the pandemic. What was previously a very small group of families, has come to represent almost 1% of school age children and philosophical reasons are no longer the main reason for choosing home education although still a common one. A rise in dissatisfaction with the school system, children's needs not being met, bullying and poor mental health of the child means that more and more parents are turning to home education not through personal beliefs on what a good education constitutes, but through the negative lense of home ed being the only other option. This doesn't mean home education won't be beneficial, I myself came to home education through similar means, but it can mean that parents are deregistering children who are already experiencing difficulties, struggles, disengagement from education, low school attendance with the accompanying stress and anxiety of the parent. When home education is not a positive choice made by the parent it leaves potential for challenges to compound and that is a genuine concern local authorities have. Ideally, home education will be a positive choice to provide an education and will have been considered and likely researched in depth before being opted for. As someone who volunteers my time to support new home educators and has done for several years (both within the UK and worldwide) there has been a clear trend since the pandemic in parents jumping first and asking questions later. This will always be a factor for some parents, and I continue to be 100% behind the fact that it is necessary in some circumstances, but the rise in supporting these families has been clear and I'm yet to know exactly what we could do better to support families. It was noted by local authorities in their interactions with new home educators during the pandemic, culminating in the state issuing additional information sheets on parents' rights and state expectations regarding home education. This came alongside an expectation that families meet with the LA and school before choosing to home educate to ensure parents understand what they are choosing and that support to provide the education is not available. These meetings were not compulsory and are still not compulsory but are now mentioned in the Keeping children safe in education guidance (2022).

Parents have a legal right to choose how their child is educated and to act in what they believe are the best interests of their child. The state has a duty to interject if they believe the child is at risk of harm or being harmed. Social care is duty bound to investigate every referral made to them and home educators are referred to social care for lots of reasons. Some of these reasons are due to a lack of understanding and training, others are genuine concerns that home education may complicate an already challenging circumstance for a child. Many of these referrals are closed very quickly if these families do not meet any threshold of potential harm and are not in need of support but they do take up precious time and can be further complicated because school staff don't necessarily have the levels of training or expertise to allow them to make deeply informed assessments. Our society says, if in doubt, report everything and then your back is covered and that remains the current ethos which personally, I think is understandable.

Services also have historic reasons for concern, especially if there were concerns surrounding the child before home education was decided upon, because almost all serious case reviews where home education was considered a factor, were with families already known to services. I always find it strange when home educators opt for a blanket denial that home educated children can be subject to abuse or harm. All children are at risk of abuse or harm, simply because they are children and vulnerable. As parents it's our job to protect them from this and the state's job to step in if we cannot or do not do so. Home educated children are not exempt from this. A significant number of children who are supported or need to be supported by social care services in general, do not come from 'bad' parents. Children who die or are seriously harmed are far lower in number when compared to the population in full and the figures shared further up confirm this. But each of those children were harmed in awful ways. Each is a tragedy. Each one is heartbreaking. Each one is anger inducing and we should *always* question if more could have been done to prevent those situations. It's also a well-known fact that we only know what we know. Many children are harmed with no one ever becoming aware. Pretending that home education is not a part of any of that is unhelpful. And while thankfully the largest number of families being supported by social care are not a part of those serious harm statistics, the reviews into how the harm was able to happen, provides us with learning as a country.

Trust between home educators and those charged with reactive safeguarding duties is also complex. While serious cases involving home education are rare, they are often high profile. An evidence-based review of the risks to children and young people who are educated at home, commissioned by the National Independent Safeguarding Board (Wales) in October 2017 identified 57 sources of UK evidence via a rapid review of literature since the year 2000. They also looked at 11 child practice reviews and serious case reviews where home education was considered a factor[13]. I don't believe it's our job to decide whether home ed *was* a factor or not. It's our job to understand how home ed has been considered a factor and appreciate how this impacts on the views of home education. I'm going to share some higher profile cases below. Please note they are difficult to read. To respect the children who were involved in these reviews and those who are now the adults dealing with the long-term trauma of these experiences, I do not mention any names

---

[13] Home education report 2017
https://safeguardingboard.wales/2017/11/23/home-education-children-report-2/

and have attempted to balance the information so that you have the main details, without too many of the traumatising details of the events.

## *Serious neglect, physical, emotional abuse date unknown.*

*This case is regarding the serious harm caused to a 9-year-old boy who had learning difficulties and autism, along with his siblings. The children were home educated. He was found, together with his siblings to be suffering from serious neglect and physical and emotional abuse. He had not been seen by any professional since the age of 14 months, was not known to the local education authority, and was not and never had been, in receipt of education, health or social care services to meet his additional needs. A belief in spirit possession had led to his parents seeking faith-based treatment for him overseas. He was the youngest of six children. The Children's parents who were arrested and charged are now serving prison sentences for child cruelty. Following a very detailed email to Childline sent by the older sibling, police and social care attended the property and removed the children into police protection. Initially the parents denied the youngest child's existence to the officers at this visit, but he was found in an upstairs room. Regarding home education, procedures were followed for the child's siblings. A visit from the home education advisor took place just over a year before the children were removed and the education was found to be suitable. At the point of rescue, all the children had multiple unmet health,* education, developmental, nutritional, and social needs. They were dressed in ill-fitting shared family clothing and lacked awareness of basic road safety. Lack of daylight had impacted on their vitamin D levels and the inability to engage in outdoor exercise had seriously limited their development of gross motor skills. The family were not known to any primary services such as social services or the police until the removal of the children.

### Manslaughter, allowing the death of a child and child cruelty 2008.

This case involves the death of a 7-year-old girl in 2008 and child cruelty to her siblings. The cause of her death was recorded as bronchial pneumonia and septicaemia with focal bacterial meningitis, and she was described as extremely malnourished with severe wasting. There was significant starvation over a period of several months and all of the surviving siblings were malnourished to a greater or lesser extent. The Children's mother and her partner (not the children's father) were convicted of manslaughter, allowing the death of a child and 5 other offences of child cruelty. While there is confusion around whether the children were ever officially deregistered to be home educated, it's clear from the evidence that this was the mother's intention, and she made this clear on many occasions. Concerns were already well documented by the time the children were being educated at home and in the case review it is made clear that there were a number of early missed opportunities for intervention. The review concluded that based on all the information, the death of the child was preventable and that while her death was the responsibility of the mother and the *adult male, had there been better assessments and effective interagency communication over a period of time it could have been prevented.*

### Sexual, physical abuse and child murder 2010

*This case involved the near decade long historic sexual abuse of a female child, the psychical abuse of her brother and the subsequent murders of their younger siblings. Their mother held positions of trust in various local authorities working in both an educational and child services capacity. She withdrew the older siblings from school to electively home educate, was a fierce advocate of home education and an advisor to other home educators at the time that the abuse was happening to the children, at the hands of her partner (not the children's father). Once she was an adult, female child came forward and disclosed the abuse to authorities in 2007. At that time the mother and partner fled to Spain with their younger daughter. The couple went on to have another child before the partner was arrested and returned to the UK in 2010 to face the charges of abuse. Not long after his arrest, the mother killed her two youngest children while in Spain and is now serving more than 30 years in a Spanish prison for their murders. The partner of the mother was convicted of the oldest female child's historic abuse in 2011 and sentenced to 16 years. He took his own life while in prison, in 2012.*

## Gross negligence 2016

*Another case being the utterly abhorrent manslaughter of an 18-year-old in 2016. His mother, sister and grandmother were all charged with his death. His mother and grandmother were found guilty of manslaughter by gross negligence and his sister was found guilty of allowing the death of her brother. The person in question weighed less than 6 stone when he died. His cause of death was identified as bronchopneumonia caused by three factors: malnutrition, immobility, and infected pressure sores. Experts stated that he had been severely malnourished for months if not years. Previous concerns around his development and risk of neglect were noted and the family supported until the case was closed. He was deregistered to be home educated shortly after starting secondary school until he was 16 and did not go into further education or employment. Home education officers did visit with the family when the victim was around 15 and nothing of concern was raised at that time. The family maintains that no one was to blame for his death, despite a clear choice by all 3 family members not to seek help for his condition earlier due to his refusal to engage in said services.*

## Chronic neglect 2011 - 2020

*This case involves the chronic neglect of a now adult female. The chronic neglect of this child took place for the majority of her childhood and has had significant and long-lasting effects on her life. In 2020 she was removed from the care of her family and placed in long term foster care under adult social care services. No charges were brought against her mother who was sectioned under the mental health act and subsequently diagnosed with a significant psychiatric condition. Concerns surrounding the child's development, presentation and learning difficulties alongside concerns around the mother's mental health and the risk of physical and emotional neglect were identified at a young age and reported appropriately with interventions attempted. The mother had a history of non-engagement with these services over time. The child had significant poor attendance throughout her school years culminating in a request for educational welfare support at which point the mother deregistered and the child became home educated from 2015. In 2016 the EHE team made a referral to social care under concerns of a lack of suitable education alongside home conditions. The child was made subject to a child protection plan in 2016. Engagement in alternative education and referrals to CAMHS were not engaged with and by 2018 although care orders were explored, due to the child's age being 16 at this point, it was decided this course of action was unlikely to be successful. She did however remain on a child protection plan until early 2019. During a home visit in 2020 it became apparent the child and mother had moved in with other family members which presented a significant risk to the child. Eventually in Aug 2020 she was taken into protective custody and was assessed as required immediate medical attention and was subsequently placed with long term foster carers.*

The case review details above show the complexity of not only how harm occurs, but also the elements that can complicate matters. Underfunded services, risk factors, mental health, educational difficulties, family situations, cultures and so much more all feed into the balance of understanding how we can help to keep children safe. Home education featured in each of these children's lives to varying extents. While it may not have been considered the primary factor in the harm they experienced, it was a feature of the lives of these children that was worthy of mention. Home education is not an exclusive club where abuse fails to happen and when the home education community bangs a drum of denial it is a cause of harm to the community within itself. Abuse, harm, and neglect happens in many circumstances and situations and home education is *not* exempt.

The responses by the state regarding these crimes and others, has caused home educators to feel criminalised for the crimes of the few. When these horrific acts of harm to children have happened, local authorities have understandably over compensated and thrown the entire balance off. In terms of how many home educated children are known to have been seriously harmed the numbers are tiny. Whether this is due to their genuinely being less harm in the community or the ability for home education to isolate the family from services, is unknown and there are arguments of both sides regarding this. What we do know is that there are children harmed on a daily basis and this is a sad and horrible truth to know. Some of these children come to be known to services and others do not. There are children attending schools who are being harmed and despite daily contact with other adults, no one has picked up on it, because despite the best efforts of all involved some children will be seriously harmed or killed. None of us want that to happen and we continue to learn from the tragedies of those who came to harm previously. Knowing this doesn't mean as a society we have adopted a view of all parents being abusive unless checks prove otherwise, and such a view would lead to significant distrust between parents and the state causing further potential harm to more children. In terms of the risk of abuse for home educated children, thorough research from all sides has been conducted over the years to ascertain if home educated children are more likely to suffer harm and the findings from all sides continue to be clear; home educated children are no more likely to suffer harm than schooled children. **No more likely** is not necessarily cause for celebration though. It doesn't mean harm doesn't happen in the community, it simply means that home educated children are as likely to suffer harm and not more likely.

## My own thoughts

How on earth do we find a balance in all of this? Well, honestly, I'm not sure. Reading through many cases reviews hasn't exactly renewed my faith in humans. We know that overreaching state intervention causes distrust and disengagement in any community. We know that dismissing the understandable concerns of professionals is unhelpful. We know that the vast majority of home educators do a wonderful job of caring for and educating their children. We know that scoffing at what professionals view as genuine concern is unhelpful. We know that LA staff pushing disproportionate safeguarding and welfare measures upon families after many have been failed by the system in the first place, is understandably met with resistance and anger. We know that this resistance is too often then seen as non-engagement or avoidance, leading to further intervention. We can see from case reviews that there is a possibility that a small proportion of abusive people, may choose to use home education as a distancing tool and while its right to have an awareness of that, it's also right that the state use the powers it already has and ensure it puts the rights of the child before all other people. It's a really sticky situation. When looking at the awful harm caused to several children over the years where home education had some level of involvement, I can appreciate why local authorities can be overzealous with their contact, but I'm not sure viewing all home educators as potentially harmful is the way to go about keeping more children safe. And on the other side, home educators being overzealous in their right to a private life and pushing the 'abuse doesn't happen in home ed' rhetoric doesn't help either.

So, what can be done? For me, I firstly think that as home educating families it is essential that we model the critical thinking skills we aim to instil in our own children around this issue. Abuse can happen anywhere and to anyone. It does and has happened within home education, just as it does and has happened in all other spaces that children exist within. Accepting this and recognising that we must do all we can to safeguard our children within our community is essential. As home educators we must recognise that we are uniquely placed to partner with authorities to gain better outcomes for all children. We are not their enemy, nor them, ours.

Secondly, given that home education has reached much higher numbers it makes sense that LA EHE teams be responsible for ensuring the quality education of their peers. We need better training for those working with children, to help with recognition that home education is a valid and legal choice, is not a safeguarding concern in and of itself and respect towards parents who are presumed to be working in the best interests of their child. We need beneficial relationships between those working with children and families.

Thirdly, we need a system that works to recognise its own faults. To accept that the reasons a child may be struggling before deregistering are not necessarily indicative of the parents' abilities and intentions, but of a system that is not accommodating far too many children. I see too many schools and LAs parroting the lofty ideals of state school being world class and suitable for all when it is very much not the case. Those families need genuine support to help make home ed work for them, or support to find a school that can better meet the child's individual needs. What they don't need is to be treated as if they are doing something wrong or dangerous or be threatened with fines and court for reaching crisis point.

Lastly and possibly most importantly, we need a well-funded social care and school system with better ratios of workers to children and a state that works to meet all articles of the CRC instead of just cherry picking the ones that best push their agenda. Reducing potential harm to children in our country means working to reduce the financial insecurity of families as a minimum. We know financial insecurity is a massive risk factor and can create a domino effect so again, this seems like a no brainer but hey, I'm no politician. When less children are being harmed by the state itself, it leaves space to support the families where situations are far more complex and provides opportunity for social care services to address complex and time sensitive cases with full focus, leading to less harm overall. And until we have a country that can genuinely put children first, we at the very least need honesty and truth in the failings, instead of every stakeholder blaming the other. (Home educators included) None of what I've shared is new information, none of my thoughts are groundbreaking. They are just one person's thoughts on how we might eventually find a way through, but it won't ever happen if we cannot learn to see the other side's concerns and value them in our decisions and actions.

*Time for a breather.*

This chapter was such a difficult one to write. As a mother it is such a heart wrenching thing to read about the harm of children, knowing there are people out there who are the worst of humanity, causing suffering. As a parent I think it's natural to want your choices to be something you can say reduces risks to your children. We want to be able to say it would never happen to us, or in a community we belong to. But the truth is, there are horrendous people in the world, and they exist in all areas of society, home education included.

But that isn't the whole story of safeguarding and harm. Protecting children is a complex thing full of so many elements and not all of these are within a parent's control or ability. When we only focus on the worst harm, we become blind to the harms that can go unnoticed for years. Domestic violence, neglect, severe mental health difficulties, insecurity and so much more. As a home education community, I believe we have to stop denying that abuse happens because until we do, we cannot work together to reduce the very harms we want to reduce. Accepting that abuse can and does happen in all areas, including home ed doesn't mean home education isn't safe and it doesn't mean we need to be monitored and scrutinised. It simply is a first step towards working with all stakeholders to make a difference. Because for me, while my parental rights are important, my children's right to be safe and free from harm as more so.

Reflect on your own thoughts and ideas that have come up around this chapter, be gentle with you as you do so, and do you know what else? Be gentle with your fellow home educators too, wherever they sit on the safeguarding argument.

# Educational outcomes of home educated people.

Can you believe we are at the end of the book already?! Let's have a look at the good old educational outcomes. It always comes up and so seemed like a good place for the last chapter, especially after the last chapter being such a difficult one. Let's dig in.

There is an unhealthy obsession with the educational outcomes of young people who were home educated, as if home education is some crazy experiment or theory that requires careful monitoring. Home education is a natural and normal approach to education. It is something that has been done for thousands of years, well before school systems came into being or this type of education was given a name. In fact, I would argue that school is the experiment considering how little time it's been around in the grand scheme of human life and learning. The first thing to note is that educational outcomes tend to relate mainly to compulsory school age. They are about what happens to students at the end of compulsory school age as a result of the objectives and aims of the educational input and the outputs (exams) of the students themselves. I find this whole area of education very restrictive despite understanding why it's supposed to be there. I do get that for improvement to happen over time, you need to be able to hypothesise, act, gather results and then review and if this was the true objective of measuring educational outcomes, I'd probably be more on board with it.

In truth, school is big business. For me, educational outcomes became a main focus, not for the benefit of pupils but for money, thanks to the Education Reform Act in 1988. What this act did was to essentially create an open market with schools competing with each other for customers (i.e., children). Families became consumers voting with their feet depending on which schools performed best. Formula funding was introduced meaning that the more pupils a school could attract, the more money it then received from the government. The theory was that 'bad' schools would then be forced to improve or close. Good old Thatcherism at its best!

Interestingly this is when the national curriculum was also introduced. Yes, my friends, the national curriculum is younger than most of us parents and yet continues to be held up as the golden child of educational outcomes. Of course, they then needed to test how well a school was doing so they could award funding and naturally that meant the introduction of national curriculum assessments and standardised assessment tests, or SATs to the rest of us. Add to this the approach that parents were now able to have elements of choice over where their children attended and well, it's the perfect recipe for the education postcode lottery that is the legacy of Margaret Thatcher's influence on education. This is not to say that Thatcher is individually responsible for the dire state of education in 2023, but my word she had quite the influence.

Thanks to Labours 'Skills and Learning Act' 2000 and then Conservative David Cameron's expansion of it via his coalition government of 2010 - 2016, we had academies introduced, allowed publicly funded schools to become academies and therefore receiving greater autonomy, more options for funding and a choice to merge with other schools and create multi academy trusts. This basically has left us with state schools that are not under the control of the local authority. Multi Academy Trusts receive funding directly from the government alongside other funding via sponsors, with low performing schools being ordered to join a MAT (multi academy trust) to help them improve. But multi academy trusts are not for profit charities so how are they big business and why would that not lead to better educational outcomes for children?

While MATs are indeed not for profit charities, they are businesses by default as opposed to state services. They are run and overseen by directors and influenced by stakeholders and trustees. Headteachers are now managers, with senior leadership teams being in charge of the day to day running of the school while all being accountable to the business stakeholders rather than the consumers (children and families). Because they are not beholden to the same rules as local authority-maintained schools, they are able to buy in educational services from for profit companies and many of those companies just happen to be linked to the MAT management, sponsors, trustees, or stakeholders. Where schools were previously competing for government funding, they are now competing for personal profits under the guise of not-for-profit charity, privatisation. Educational outcomes are not about the individual life chances of a child leaving the education system and their future but about lining the pockets of those in charge in the present. The current government has an aim to change all local authority funded schools into academies by 2030, giving us a privatised education system that is focused on making money for its stakeholders, rather than improving the life chances of its consumers, in less than a decade. So, while yes, I do believe educational outcomes are important and valuable information, it's not for the same reasons as those who oppose home education.

It's worth noting that while Academies are bound by the same duty to admit children if their school is named on an EHCP (education health care plan) there are ways around this if they can show that the school is not suitable for the child or if admitting the child would significantly interfere with the education of other students. This same duty applies to local authority-controlled schools too. However, this duty does not apply to children without an EHCP. Keep in mind that there were around 1.5million children identified as SEN in 2022 and only around 450,000 of those children held an EHCP. Some schools, academies and multi academy trusts are inclusive and others are not. And whether a school is under local authority control or not, when your funding or (nonprofit) profits are made up of your performance as a school, there will always be ways to increase your educational outcomes. There is evidence that as SEN students reach GCSE level, they are removed from school rolls, both in schools and academies. Children who exhibit challenging behaviour are excluded. Some children are unofficially excluded, moved to referral units that are not attached to that school's performance data or even simply off rolled. This is the kind of sickening behaviour that happens when the education system is incentivised by performance figures, by educational outcomes. Children who need greater support to receive the education they are entitled to by law, are shoved from pillar to post, parents are pushed into a corner to deregister, or children are excluded on flimsy grounds. As long as they are someone else's problem that's all that matters. This is not the kind of education system anyone deserves and why the educational outcomes of less than 1% of all school age children feels really rather irrelevant when faced with the truth.

## But what are the outcomes of home ed children?

Despite everything I've shared about why educational outcomes aren't what we think they are, you are still going to want to know about home ed children. Maybe you think I've spoken about why outcomes are pants to distract away from home education outcomes being horrendous. After all, the government rhetoric is that they just don't know anything about these poor children who are clearly being deprived because well, they don't have the data to say otherwise. You've probably read the news over the years about this invisible group of children no one knows anything about. What's actually true is that the outcomes of home-ed children aren't compatible with the media and government campaigns and so they dismiss the data that does exist. The other issue is that the data we do have on the educational outcomes of home educated children is not comparable to the data they hold on to school leaving children. This is because the data on educational outcomes for schools is based on GCSE results, progress 8 and the destinations of students after school. So, how many children gain GCSEs, how many pass English and maths, how the school performs in terms of the 8 GCSEs / technical qualifications in the progress 8 tables and whether these children go on to A levels, college, work or do apprenticeships.

In contrast home educated children are not obliged to take GCSEs or be a part of progress 8 league tables. Although many do take GCSEs, these are primarily taken as private or independent candidates in schools or exams centres. The results of these home educated children are then mixed with all other private candidates making comparable outcome data almost impossible. Added to this is the complication that home educated children (or anyone) can take exams whenever they are ready, and this complicates matters. In fact, the oldest person to pass a maths GCSE was Derek Skipper at the age of 92 in 2022. Exams are also often taken over a longer period of time, spreading several exams over 3, 4 or 5 years as well as at different times of year. Therefore, any comparable results would be spread over years, rather than one cohort once a year. Another factor that affects the data is access to exams. Home educated families pay for exam costs themselves and are responsible for finding an exam centre, choosing a course, and paying any associated costs. This means that many home educators will focus on the exams a child is interested in, requires and is more likely to pass, whereas in school you will have thousands of children often taking 8 or more exams with varying success as although they may succeed in gaining a grade, some of these will be not classed as a pass (above a 4) due to students being entered into exams they do not require or are less confident in. Anecdotally home educators tend to do well in exams but there is always an underlying question of whether this is down to the child's inherent ability and the 1 to 1 support that home education brings, less stress as not taking as many exams at once, the fact they take fewer exams in general and so can focus more deeply, that they can spread them out over years or a mix of all of the above.

## So, what do we know?

Well, we know that home ed is simply not comparable to school for a start and we know that the metrics used to report school based educational outcomes of post 16-year-olds cannot be used to measure the same data in home educators. But we do have a wonderful amount of research that measures outcomes of home education in ways that make sense. These measurements are based on attainment of skills over time, social skills, abilities, self-image, confidence, independence, what they go on to do with their lives, and how satisfied in their educational experience they are. Much of the research into home education continues to be primarily driven by American researchers, however we do have a growing body of research in the UK. I will discuss some of this research further down however as this book is not a research paper, let's begin with the all-important individual outcomes of children and adults who have been home educated.

Educational outcomes of home educated people survey.

As part of this book, I surveyed people who were home educated and the parents of people who had been home educated. The aim of this survey was to provide a space for home educators and those who were home educated, to share their experiences on the outcomes that matter to them. The educational and societal outcomes of home educated people is a difficult area of research, due to the variety of ways in which home education may take place but the responders did not disappoint, providing reflective, considered, and detailed information on their experiences.

**Background of the home education**

All those surveyed were from the UK and the home education took place in the UK. 75% of those responding were parents with 25% being people who were home educated. 44.4% were home educated for 1 - 4 years, 11.1% for 5 - 8 years and 44.4% were home educated for their entire compulsory school age. The most common form of home education style amongst those surveyed was unschooling / self-directed education with the second most common being semi structured.

Responders shared some of their favourite things about home education.

*"Being part of my children's childhood, doing things together as a family and the close relationships that brought us, seeing my children blossom in their own unique ways, seeing my two children being really close as siblings."*

*"Flexibility, freedom and family! As a family we are close, and everyone has had the chance to develop in their own time and in their own ways. I wouldn't have changed it for the world."*

*"Home education allowed for significant exploration of my own interests, with my learning being focused around what I enjoyed as well as my 'extracurriculars', something that helped me to develop a more robust sense of self at an early age."*

Challenges were also shared too such as *"The constant-ness. Four children relatively close in age, living rurally and with no close family support for most of the time, plus a husband who frequently worked away when they were young meant it was very full on. The responsibility is all on you which can be daunting too." "The constant messy house"* and *"Not getting a break"*.

**Educational outcomes**

50% of those surveyed noted qualifications of passes in GCSEs, iGCSEs, BTECs and functional skills before the end of compulsory school age. Of those who gained qualifications before the end of compulsory school age, 75% achieved further qualifications or are currently studying for qualifications such as BTEC, NVQ, A levels, degree, PhD. 25% went out to work full time and continue to be in employment.

The other 50% did not complete any qualifications before the end of compulsory school age. Of those who did not take qualifications before the end of compulsory school age,

50% are continuing to be home educated and 50% went on to gain qualifications in their chosen areas of study, either within further education or employment.

100% of responders advised that education, employment, or training was continued post 16.

**Holistic outcomes**

100% of parent respondents felt that home education had helped with their child's confidence, sense of self and independence and 100% felt that home education had achieved what they set out for it to achieve. One notable comment shared by a parent was *"If you'd have asked me before March 2020, I'd have said I wanted my child to have the same doors open to him at 16 that he would have had if he went to school. It definitely achieved that - he achieved 10 GCSEs/IGCSEs - lowest a 6. Standing on a windswept, rainy beach the day after the first Covid lockdown and exam cancellations were announced I realised that none of that mattered. What I wanted was for my child to get to 16 physically and mentally healthy. In that sense I think it achieved it too. Don't get me wrong the exam cancellations were not a walk in the park but we valued so much the flexibility and freedom home ed gave to decide what was best for him. It also gave us a relaxed approach to the GCSEs themselves - grabbed opportunities to sit when they came up and didn't really worry about the grades."*

Another parent shared *"It was a leap of faith at times but everything I hoped would come from it has done so. She is secure in herself, has a great attitude to learning, will dive deeply into the things that interest her and work hard at the things she has decided for herself are important."*

These views were echoed by those who were home educated with statements such as:

*"School had stripped any confidence that I had, it was my parents that built me backup and gave me the confidence to function as an adult."*

*"I believe that home education did help me with my sense of self. This is because home education allowed me to develop my sense of self primarily apart from the significant influence of others, whether that influence originated from social media or from my peers. Although I likely was influenced by some of my peers, through interactions with them, I do not believe that this influence significantly impacted the development and strength of my sense of self, as home education allowed me to develop my sense of self in a somewhat separate environment reducing the significance of the influence."*

*"I learnt how to be an adult and look after myself, something I believe I would not have learnt in school."*

*"In a way, I think home education could have had a detrimental impact on my life skills, as I'd rarely caught a train on my own or even just been on my own before college. That said, the sense of independence that comes from not needing to always follow a teacher's say-so meant that I adapted to the new circumstances quickly. Home education, in my specific case, didn't necessarily give me*

*any specific life skills, but it gave me the tools I needed to learn them on my own."*

*"To me, being an independent member of society is quite simply - it's someone who can contribute to society while not having to rely on someone else. I definitely think that home education has equipped me with the skills for this - I might even say I'm already half-way there! - through cultivating confidence, sense of self, and independence. It has also allowed me to develop many helpful skills that will allow me to not only support myself, but also be able to contribute to society."*

When asked if there was anything additional, they wanted to share, one young person shared some wise words that I think is beautiful to end with:

"Being home educated is often said to set you apart from most people. For me, however, that seems to be the opposite of what being home educated does. It doesn't actually impede friendships with school educated people - there's certainly always something to talk about - but it does give you a community that most people just don't get. Even if I've never met you, if you've been home educated, I have a connection to you. We share something really big, that's shaped our lives in incredible ways, and I find that incredibly special. For me, that's probably the most wonderful part of home education."

## Other research into home education

In an article named Home Education: A Successful Educational Experiment? By Simone de Hoogh[14] of PowerWood, de Hoogh shares excellent references to research both from the UK and further afield. In their article they share the below findings.

Studies confirm that home educated children on average achieve higher intellectual scores than their school going age-mates, regardless of whether the parents follow an existing (school) curriculum or whether education is child-led (ACTP, 1997-2001; Calvery et al., 1992; Galloway, 1995; Ray, 1994; Ray, 1997; Rothermel, 2002; Rudner, 1999; Sutton & Oliveira, 1995). Only Tipton 1990 reports no difference in the scores of home educated children.

Some studies have even found that the lead of home educated children can be considerable. Six-year-olds had a lead of one schoolyear, which increased during their school career to four years at the age of fourteen. This means that an average fourteen-year-old home educated child is comparable – in terms of schooling – to an eighteen-year-old who goes to school (Ray, 1994; Ray 1997; Rothermel, 2002; Rudner, 1999)

Moreover, home educated children continue to perform better after secondary school than school-taught children;

---

[14]Home education: A successful educational experiment? Simone de Hoogh
https://www.powerwood.org.uk/results-home-education/

for example, it turns out that they cope better with the transition to university (Lattibeaudiere, 2000).

Home educated children prove to have no fewer social skills than children who have gone to school. Several studies show that homeschooled children are on average socially more skilled and more mature than school children (Smedley, 1992). As adults, they report more influence on their surroundings and on their lives, and they have more active social lives than adults who have gone to school (Ray, 2004b).

Their satisfaction with their parents' decision to home educate is shown by the fact that in one study (n=807), 74% of the home educated adults also home educated their children (Ray, 2004b).

Studies also show that home educated children develop a more positive self-image than their out-of-the-home-schooled peers (Taylor, 1986). Within developmental psychology, the behaviour of a child with a 'stable attachment' towards the parents is seen as most healthy and adaptive. Stably attached children use their parents as a safe base from which to explore the world. Although stable attachment is not a guarantee of a good mental health, it is a protecting factor during times of trouble (Mönks & Knoers, 2004).

A long-term study in Great Britain also showed that working-class children who receive home education scored better than school-going children of professional middle-class parents and that for home educated children gender differences in the exam results disappear (Rothermel, 2002).

It seems as if schools are less able to compensate than are home educating parents, and thus working-class children are, relatively speaking, better off being home-educated (Basham, 2001; Blok, 2002; Ray, 1997, 2004a; Rothermel, 2002).

Learning difficulties and behavioural problems often seem to be school related (Armstrong, 2000, p.7). It is therefore not surprising that behavioural problems occur less in home educated children (Shyers, 1992). Within school, the most effective way to approach learning difficulties is a one-on-one approach (Woolfolk, 2004, p. 126).

Research shows that learning programs tuned towards the individual, flexibility, one-on-one approaches, and the fact that home education is very efficient, makes it an excellent choice for special pupils (Ray, 2004b, p.11).

Home education makes it possible to individualise instruction, respecting the principles of a good education for high-ability children. Home education gives all highly and differently gifted children a chance to flourish in a way that is tuned to their unique needs (Rivero, 2002, p.182-184)

Moreover, home educated highly gifted children with learning disabilities (twice exceptional or DME Dual and Multi Exceptional) are self-confident students, and although their academic skills may develop at uneven rates, they have usually achieved academic proficiency by high school (Ensign, 2000, p.157)

I'd highly recommend reading the research provided above as some of it is really interesting! To conclude, the end product of all education should be that the person who has received the education is more knowledgeable, has gained useful skills and that they are able to live as a functioning, independent member of society. Personally, I think that's a pretty minimal aim and an aim that the majority of home educators surpass without breaking a sweat. The realities of home education may be very different to the expectations, but my word the journey is worth every stressful, full on, white knuckled moment especially when you see your now adult children thriving in the world as the amazing human beings they are.

# I don't want to read the book, where is the cheat sheet?

Below is a handy little collection of frequently asked questions for when you just need the answer, without needing to read pages of a book. Almost like a TL, DR section. Let's dig in.

## Q. Is home education legal?

Absolutely! (In the UK anyway!) Home education is legal in all 4 countries that make up the UK. As we have devolved nations for things like education, the guidelines, and laws around how you can home educate may differ for each country so its super important to look up the guidelines for your country.

## Q. Who do I need to ask for permission to home educate?

You don't need to request permission in any of the 4 UK countries. However, in Scotland there is a consent process if the child is currently in a school and in all 4 countries you may need to gain consent if your child is in a special school paid for by the LA . Because of this the answer depends on your country and circumstances, look up the guidelines for your country.

## Q. Who do I need to tell if I decide to home educate?

This will depend on where you are at. If your child has never been to school and you've chosen home education as a first choice, there is currently no obligation to inform anyone. If you are wanting to remove your child from school to begin home education, the process differs dependant on the country, but in England you will be expected to provide a deregistration letter informing the school that you are now home educating in line with s.7 of the education act 1996. They then inform the local authority.

## Q. What if the school says they won't let me home educate?

The legal responsibility to ensure a child is provided with an education falls to the parents, not the school or the state. This means that schools cannot legally refuse to deregister a child if a parent has issued the school with an instruction to deregister. The pupil registration regulations make clear what the responsibilities of the school is and you can refer the school to it.

## Q. Does the LA provide funding and resources to home ed?

In short no. The local authority has a duty to identify children who are not receiving an education, but they do not have a duty to support home educators. Some local authorities are able to offer access to discounted resources or helping to put you in touch with local home educators, but they receive no funding to support home educators and it is not their responsibility to fund home ed either. When you become home educated parents become fully responsible for any financial obligations.

## Q. Does the LA pay for exams?

Again, in short no. The financial obligations for any associated costs such as exams, falls to the parent. There are a couple of local authorities who are able to provide minimal funds towards exams but these are very rare.

## Q. Can I home educate if my child has an EHCP? Or is in a specialist school?

You can yes. But do check the most current legislation around deregistration. At the time of writing this book,  If your child has an EHCP in England and attends a mainstream school, deregistration can be carried out as normal. This would then trigger a review of the EHCP which is separate to the deregistration itself. You do not currently need consent. If your child is in a special school that is paid for by the local authority, you will need to seek consent from the LA to remove the child from the school roll. This is not seeking consent to home educate, but to remove the child from the school itself (for any reason).


## Q. What if home ed doesn't work out. Can my child go back to school?

Absolutely.  If for whatever reason you feel your child need to be in school instead of home educated, you can contact the admissions department and begin an application to find a school for your child. In some areas, if you deregistered recently, you may be expected to return your child to the same school they left. You may also have to wait some time before a space becomes available if you are wanting a specific school.

## Q. Is there someone I need to report to? Like a teacher who checks that I'm doing it right?

No. Parents are responsible for ensuring their child receives a suitable education, no one else. The local authority may contact you to inquire about the education and its always sensible to respond to them, but this is to help them discharge their duty towards children who are not receiving an education. There are several ways you may wish to communicate with the local authority when they make inquiries, head over to chapter 2, page 21. But no, there are not any termly check ins with a teacher or anyone else. The responsibility is the parents.

**Q. I'm scared of the local authority.**

Why? The staff at the local authority are normal people with jobs to do. In terms of the people, you would be interacting with, these are staff members who are tasked with identifying children who are not receiving an education. They do this via informal inquiries into your child's education to see if your child is their remit or not. It's really important that you inform yourself of the EHE guidelines and get confident in your responsibilities and theirs. Knowledge is power.

**Q. I'm no good at writing things for officials.**

No one is expecting you to. You are not a teacher and are not expected to write like one. What you are expected to do is to be able to speak about the learning your child has been engaging in and what you can see they've achieved. Speaking in layman's terms is very much expected of a home ed parent and no parent should be made to feel that they are doing a poor job, just because they don't use education speak in their communications.

**Q. I'm worried I'm not cut out for this and don't want to fail my child.**

I'm not sure I know many home educating parents who could say they felt cut out for home education before starting it either. It's very normal to be worried about home ed and not wanting to fail your child. After all, home ed is outside of mainstream education and often jars with us when we've been through the education system ourselves! My top tip for wobbles is to always go back to basics. Why are you doing home ed? What are you hoping it provides? How does your child learn best? Are they happy, healthy, and growing? Do more of all of that.

## Q. What if they don't socialise enough?

Children are individuals just like anyone else. Some children enjoy being around others lots, and other children enjoy their own company, just like us adults. The idea that socialising for children is being forced to associate with 30 other children their own age daily for 6 hours, is old news.

In social sciences socialisation comes in two main forms. Primary and secondary. Primary Socialisation happens in a child's immediate family in their home. These are the first types of behaviours that happen for all children and are the building blocks of wider social experiences. Primary socialisation gives children access to your own personal culture, religion, social styles, views of the world, approaches to challenges.

Secondary Socialisation happens outside of the home. This is the process of learning appropriate behaviour in the wider community via contact with people who have different experiences, views, cultures, religions, approaches. Secondary Socialisation is what people are concerned with when it comes to home education. Most commonly secondary socialisation occurs in school. It's not about the opportunity to socialise with other children, it's about the opportunity to learn the social norms of our general society within the setting. School socialisation most typically is about conditioning children in the factory model of work. The premise is for children to learn a top down approach to authority and hierarchy, with all the rules around class structure that come with it, so that they will move into a work arena of the same set up. Its premise and overall purpose hasn't changed since the industrial revolution. Without it, children may become free thinkers, agents of non-conformity and may wish for more than becoming a cog in the machine, questioning the worker bee set up. This is seen as a genuine danger to the way our society works. Your child is likely receiving plenty of appropriate socialising, it's just not the kind that children receive in school.

**Q. I'm not brainy enough to teach. I failed my GCSEs. I'm not a teacher.**

Good news! You don't need to be teacher, you don't need qualifications and you don't need to be brainy either (whatever that means). Do you know what you do need? The availability to be present for your children and help them to find the things they need, to get where they are wanting to go. Home educators are facilitators of education, not teachers. No good at maths? No problem, learn alongside your child. No good at geography? No problem, learn alongside your child. Your children don't need you to have the answers to anything, they need you to be able to say, 'I don't know, let's find out!'.

**Q. What if I can't afford it?**

One of the great things about home ed is that it can be as expensive or as low cost as you need it to be. Libraries are your friend. Free home ed meets are your best friend, museums, historical sites are amazingly low cost. The biggest expense for me is the increase in food costs and petrol for the car. We don't have lots of fancy subscriptions, tutors, classes, or courses. We choose these very carefully, make use of free trials or discounted costings via wonderful places like Pop art. In real terms home ed can often mean a restriction around how much money is coming in and so it is definitely something to consider carefully, but for many of us we make it work because it's what is necessary.

## Q. I have to work, can I still home ed?

Many families work and home ed. For some families that means both parents working part time and juggling home ed around that, for others its one parent working full time and the other staying home to home ed. For single families it can mean working hours that best suit the family and then home ed working within that, with support from benefits. Home education doesn't excuse you from working when claiming financial support, but that doesn't mean you will be expected to work full time either. Some families work from home, others with older children work out of the house for set hours. It is important to note that while there is no laws around what age a child can be left home alone, the child should always be considered safe and able to keep themselves safe if something were to happen. The NSPCC has good advice around this.

## Q. Can we have holidays in term time? Can we go out during the day?

You can have holidays whenever you wish and one of the perks of home ed is cheaper holidays during term time! The EHE guidelines make clear that home educating families are just as entitled to reasonable holidays as schooled children and that you do not need to follow school based term times in any way. You can absolutely go out during the day. Home education doesn't mean 'at home' it simply means educated not in school. We are out in our community daily and so are most other home educators.

## Q. Do home educators have to do SATs and GCSEs?

SATs relate to school performance not children and only apply to schools so no, SATs are not required for home educators. In fact, no exams or certifications are compulsory. Home ed children can take GCSEs or other qualifications whenever they wish, be that at 11 or 100, or choose not to take any. Home edders are not bound by the restrictions of the school based timeline for education.

**Q. Can I home educate more than one child?**

Yes, you can. You can home educate all of your children if that is what feels best for your family. I've home educated all 4 of my children at various points. Some of that time was all of them together and at other points I had one child in school. It's entirely possible to home educate different ages and stages of development and this is especially true if you take an interest led or self-directed approach.

**Q. What about school related immunisations and checks?**

Despite the name, the school nurse service is responsible for all children of school age, including home educators. You can always contact the school nurse in your area for things such as arranging immunisations or any checks you feel your child may need. This is an opt in service like Health visitors and so you can choose to use the service or not. Your LA website should have details of your school nurse, or you could also ask your GP practice.

**Q. Do I have to use tutors?**

No. Tutors aren't needed or necessary unless you want to use them. I would always recommend making use of the home education community, before paying for expensive tutors. If you can afford tutors and feel that is the best way to ensure your child is provided with an education, you should of course make use of them but they are not a service you must use or need to use, to enable a suitable education for your child.

**Q. My teen hated school and would rather go out to work. Can they do that instead?**

Simple answer, no. We have child labour laws and regulations for good reason and the regulations are clear on what kinds of work children of compulsory school age can and can't do. All children should be receiving an education that takes up a significant amount of their time until at least the end of compulsory school age (The last Friday in June within the academic year the child turns 16) Child 13 and over are able to work and volunteer part time within specific regulations and I highly recommend that you make yourself aware of these regulations on the government website and your Las website. The beauty of home education is that is doesn't need to look anything like school and therefore even a teen who hated school can thrive and enjoy home education.

**Q. Where can I find the curriculum I should follow or work my child should be doing?**

There is no specific curriculum you should follow nor is there specific work your child should be doing. In fact, home educated children don't have to do any 'work' either! Crazy, eh? I would recommend you read chapter 3 and chapter 8 to assist you with better understanding what home education can look like for your family!

## Q. Can I home educate if I, or my child is neurodivergent / disabled / has mental health issues?

You can! And as an ND parent to ND and disabled children, I am a huge advocate of home ed in exactly these circumstances. Remember, the school curriculum and school system were designed by neurotypical / non-disabled people for neurotypical / non-disabled children. The accommodations that are made via the SEND system are to 'help' those children access the NT curriculum/ system. The accommodations are not there to provide a curriculum/system that makes sense to ND brains or disabled children's needs. That's why home ed works really well when you tailor and individualise the child's education to them- in whatever way that needs to look for them. This benefits you as well. I know for me, a huge drain on my own mental health and energy levels was having to deal with the constant fall outs around school too. As home edders, we can flow with each day as it happens and can adjust as and when needed, meaning we can accommodate all of our needs.

## Q. Can I do home education part time instead?

This is called flex schooling and is possible, but it depends on a schools discretion. If flexi schooling is agreed, your child would remain the responsibility of the school and would attend school part time and be home educated the rest of the time. While this can work for some families, others find the restrictions around attending school too challenging to manage. It is also something that only tends to be agreed to in primary education and even then, it is rare.

## Q. How will I know I'm doing it right?

Is your child learning new things? Is your child progressing in their understanding of anything? Is your child happy, engaged, health and strong? Is your child surprising you with their thoughts or questions? If the answer to most of these is yes, you are probably doing it 'right'. (What does doing it right mean?) Maybe have a nose at chapter3, 4 and 8.

## Q. Where can I get support?

Fellow home educators are your best source of support. They are the ones in the trenches doing it alongside you or have been where you are and are genuinely fonts of knowledge! You can find them online via Facebook groups, and other social media and in person at local meets.

Okay that's your lot! For anything else, read the book!

# Further Reading

Please find below some of the amazing books, bloggers, and other stuff that I highly recommend.

**Sir Ken Robinson** - Anything by the wonderful Sir Ken Robinson, such as his world famous Ted talk: *Do schools kill creativity?* And also *Changing educational paradigms.*

**Ross Mountney** - Books such as *Learning without school* and *A home education notebook.*

**Julie Bogart** - *The Brave Learner: Finding Everyday Magic in Homeschool* and *Raising critical thinkers.*

**Alan Thomas and Harriet Patterson** - Books and research by either of these wonderful people are amazing.

**Dr Naomi Fisher** - *Changing our minds* and *A different way to learn.*

**Dr Ross Greene** - All of Dr Greene's work is wonderful such as *The explosive child* and *Raising human beings.*

**Alfie Kohn** - *Unconditional Parenting* and *Punished by rewards.*

**Peter Gray** – *Free to learn.*

**Stark raving dad** – An amazing blog and podcast from an unschooling family

**Happiness is here** – A wonderful Australian home ed blog.

**Eliza Fricker** – *Can't not won't* and her wonderful blog Missing the mark.

**Home Education For All (H.E.F.A)** – Last but not least, HEFA, the national home education support group on Facebook that I happen to admin on!

# Acknowledgements

Woah, you got all the way to the end! (either that, or you've flipped to the end for the cheat sheet and found this page)

Regardless of how you ended up here, I for one am thankful to you. Thank you for digging in and going on this journey with me and thank you for trusting me to say things as they are in my world, regardless of what they look like in yours.

To my children, Thank you to each of you for being my patient and generous teachers on this journey. It's not always easy and I'm not always the easiest student but you handle my ineptitude with compassion and kindness and I am grateful to each of you for it. What amazing human beings you are.

Thank you to my husband for his everlasting cheerleading and for always asking the questions I don't always want to hear but need to. Thank you for how hard you work outside the home, so that I can focus on the hard work inside of it.

Thank you to my closest friends for their unrelenting support, encouragement and counsel and special thanks' to my home ed family: Pip, Paula, Nikki, Issy, Joanna, Sam, Jules, Nicci, Hannah, Elly, Katie, Sarah, Katy, Kerrie, Nat, Natalia, Louise, Clare and so many more for never being too busy to listen, ask questions, proofread, edit, debate, but mostly for their patience in correcting my inability to add punctuation to anything. I love you all.

And to you, dear reader. Thank you for taking this journey with me. I hope it's one you return to often and find comfort from.

From this home ed home to yours —

Travel well, make lots of mistakes and learn beautiful things from it all.


And a final little confession to you all:

We're all just winging it.

Printed in Great Britain
by Amazon